T0194703

RARE ORDER
and **RULES**
in **CHAOS**
of **LOTTERY**
OUTCOMES

RARE ORDER
and **RULES**
in **CHAOS**
of **LOTTERY**
OUTCOMES

YURY GOLDYREV

RARE ORDER AND RULES IN CHAOS
OF LOTTERY OUTCOMES

Author Credits: Yury Goldyrev

iUniverse books may be ordered through booksellers or by contacting:

iUniverse
1663 Liberty Drive
Bloomington, IN 47403
www.iuniverse.com
1-800-Authors (1-800-288-4677)

ISBN: 978-1-5320-8103-3 (sc)
ISBN: 978-1-5320-8111-8 (e)

Print information available on the last page.

iUniverse rev. date: 08/31/2019

To Derek Scarpelli from Canada,
Mihail Kondaurov and Danil Panfilov from Russia,
my strict critics but most helpful friends.

INTRODUCTION

Dear Reader!

Thank you for just holding this small book about my lotto experience in your hands and looking through its pages deciding if it's worth buying it or not.

It is unique because in it you'll follow my way into the appealing world of different kinds of my country's and your national lotteries filled with my shrewd observations, discoveries and achievements, my own abbreviated wheeling matrixes (AWMs), my Method of Gathering (MOG), as I called it nearly 35 years ago, and PROG, as its graphic, very convenient and colored PC programme. The last two are all that you need to start hitting your winning numbers (WNs).

And the sandglass is the right image that I saw in my mind for the two parts of the book, with the first part LOTTO MARATHON, meaning all the years of my lotto activity, and the second part LOTTO SAFARI, which is my lottery penetration in summers.

Most of us can say that we owe our success to our relatives or ancestors. I am not an exception in this way and I ought to say a few words about the ones who were behind me.

Many years ago I found out that the lottery side of my life had its roots in the second half of the 18th century. I didn't know anything about it until one day, in 1984, my uncle Basil, a WWII veteran, drew my attention to a page in a Physics textbook.

It was not a current school textbook of the time. But for many years it had been very popular among teachers and all people interested in Physics because it was brilliantly written by Perelman, a great Physics popularizer of the 1930s. In the section 'Perpetuum Mobile' (Latin) the author pictured a "permiak"-peasant Lavrentiy Goldyrev from a rural area, Permskiy Region, not far from Moscow, the capital of Russia. Lavrentiy had invented his own Perpetual Motion Machine and was demonstrating it in his shed to a Moscow journalist who then reported on it in his article in a capital's magazine.

For me the most essential key-words from the article were "balls" and their "rotating" that drove Lavrentiy's machine into action. Comparing their round shape to the thick round black spots inside my wheeling matrixes I recognized the similarities between our mechanisms. And one more thing strengthened me in my confidence that I am Lavrentiy's descendant. My aunt Elizabeth recalled once that among our ancestors there was a man nicknamed "Permiak Salted Ears".

The two proofs were enough for me to be grateful to Lavrentiy and my uncle Basil who, himself, was a born do-it-yourself handyman and an electrician who the rest of his life before his death had been inventing and experimenting on an electric energy accumulator with a steel fly-wheel.

So, as you can guess now, I was doomed to be kind of an inventor, too.

As for my long lotto practice itself, it was not so smooth and triumphant as my lotto findings and the development of my own lotto system.

The collapse of the USSR, the Union of Soviet Socialist Republics, in which my compatriots and me lived until June 12, 1991 and turning it into the Russian Federation with 14 independent states around, resulted in rather long periods when there were either no lotteries in the country or I couldn't afford to play them.

Besides, duties and obligations of being a parent and a teacher often distracted me from my next notepad with the results of previous draws and all the notes of my observations next to them over what numbers were going to hit.

I am not a programmed robot either—though in this respect I wish I were — and there were weeks and months during which I simply put down the winning numbers without analyzing the trends and, oh my God, tore my hair off my head when some Great Event, or as I call it SUPERGATHERING, occurred and I used to phone my two friends, the members of our lotto syndicate, and we discussed the draw and regretted having lost the brilliant opportunity.

You can agree with me that playing your national lottery is fun and cannot be that kind of your pastime you should devote all your spare minutes to. If you do, however, and are strongly determined to win, you should be well organized, absolutely confident, excited, mentally flexible and disciplined and, at last, hardy like a long distance runner and, above all, you must learn how to win scientifically from an honest and friendly lottery expert like me.

And finally, I'd like to quote my classmate Mike's attitude to my lottery pastime:

"Expense per month = X rur/usd/euro/etc.

Income per month = Y rur/usd/euro/etc.

1. If Y = X, it's just a hobby.
2. If Y > X, it's a useful hobby.
3. If Y >> X, it's a business and it's serious"

Mihail is a physicist and a C++ programmer. It was he who wrote the PROG using my algorithm.

So, at applying your efforts to your national lotteries the task is always the only one: to turn your hobby into your business when you have already come to this stage.

CONTENTS

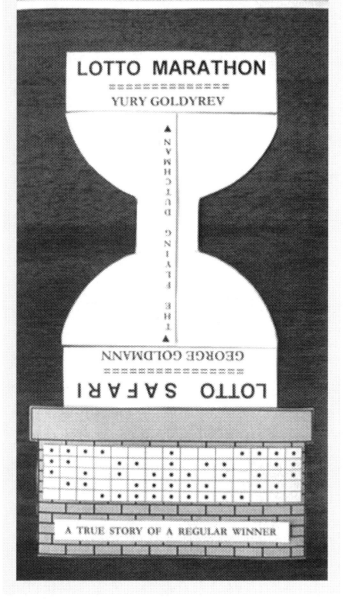

PART 1

LOTTO MARATHON

YURY GOLDYREV

THE FLYING DUTCHMAN

GEORGE GOLDMANN

LOTTO SAFARI

A TRUE STORY OF A REGULAR WINNER

BRIEF COMMENTS ON THE SIMILAR NET MATERIALS

with a few eBay credentials on my Lotto Manual.

If you are a player with enough lotto experience and quite many wins, you can skip the chapter and start reading the next chapter of the book or, perhaps, even from the middle of the book, from the description of the PROG, as by this day, I am nearly sure, there haven't been any lotto secrets left.

But if you are a newcomer, don't ignore this part to get into the core of your lottery prediction.

The section was written in 2006 for my eBay lotto manual *THE PROVEN LOTTO SYSTEM* that I (**zvezdoboy 99** eBay login) and my partner Danil (with his seller's login **russiantimes**) from Novosibirsk, a city-center of Siberian science, started selling on eBay. Danil created a pdf version of the manual, called it **Great LOTTO LOTTERY SYSTEM WIN MONEY pdf book** and I allowed him to sell it from his store, too. I sold about 10 copies from my eBay store with this positive and highly emotional feedback:

► *"what a bargain!!! hands down the best lotto info on e-bay a superb report!!!!"*

Buyer:hackable (Feedback score 67, Blue star icon) 10-Feb-07, 06:30

The manual, despite the fact that it was without PROG description, was on eBay for more than 7 years bringing Danil only positive feedbacks. Here is three of them:

► *"PERFECT!! THANK YOU!!"*

Buyer:blumen-orchdee (Feedback score 371, Green star icon) 26-Nov-09, 23:08

► *"Simply the best, thank you…"*

Buyer:elcapopr (Feedback score 232, Green star icon) 27-Nov-09, 20:59

► *"Great item and fast shipping. Thank you. 4 of 6 in first try"*

Buyer:nestordiaz (Feedback score 864, Purple star icon) 29-Jan-10, 02:38

Revising the content of the section for this new book, I see that it is not outdated because the thematical problems of such materials are always the same.

Well, before starting writing my lotto manual I downloaded and looked through the following e-books and sites I found on eBay and the Internet.

HONEST LOTTO SYSTEM, from www.honestlotto.com by Ken Silver

FREE 1000WEEKSLOTTO e-book, from the Australian e-Bay

ABOUT SYNDICATES, from www.lottery-syndicate-world.com

SYSTEM X, an e-book I purchased on the English e-Bay

GAIL HOWARD'S WHEELING SYSTEMS, from www.smartluck.com

www.lottostrategies.com, a Canadian site with the personalized methods of lotto analysis.

All of them were rather informative and helpful, particularly for me as an ESL writer, but in none of them I discovered what you'll find in this work—THE ORIGINAL OBJECTIVE METHOD OF PREDICTING CERTAIN AND SOMETIMES ALMOST ALL THE WINNING NUMBERS IN THE FUTURE DRAW ON THE BASIS OF THE PREVIOUS RESULTS, IRRESPECTIVE OF THE BALL MANUFACTURE OR/AND MACHINE DESIGN.

INCREDIBLE? BUT IT DOES TAKE PLACE
AND I AM GOING TO PROVE IT!

Let's read what their authors tell us about the predicting.

A New Zealander KEN SILVER on his interview page:

"I found that ...no-one had actually come up with a way to predict a win from past draws... It simply told me this:that no-one can actually predict winning numbers through analyzing and extrapolating past result".

The University guys from Australia begin their introduction:

"Are some lottery numbers better than others? Absolutely! Can anyone predict the six winning numbers? Absolutely not.–BUT– By modeling what actually happens in Lottery Draws you can significantly improve your chances".

With them are the LOTTERY-SYNDICATE folks in their technical aside:

"There is a whole industry built around the theory of hot and cold numbers—balls which people believe are less or more likely to be drawn... they look at past results to help predict future results. In terms of just the maths, this is rubbish of course. Personally we don't give much credit to the theory. It would likely take many thousands, if not hundreds of thousands of draws to begin to see such trends. And that assumes that the balls or machines are not replaced! It also assumes that wear and tear doesn't change those imperfections too!"

And these are their opponents from SYSTEM X:

"In the theory all numbers from 1 to 49 have the same statistical probability of being drawn. In practice however, most lotteries

develop numbers that have a higher than average appearance rate (Hot numbers), and correspondently a lower than average appearance rate (Cold numbers) ".

On the GAIL HORWARD'S site we can come across this:

"In lotto number handicapping we analyze the past action of the winning numbers to help us determine which numbers have the greatest probability of being drawn. Lottery numbers are randomly drawn. But randomly drawn numbers form patterns that are to a certain extent predictable".

The Canadian lotto experts believe *that you should use past results of the games in your personalized analysis and they give definitions of 21 analytical algorithms, among which they especially recommend the two most valuable ones:"Hot-Cold Trend Analysis and Elapse Time Trend Analysis".*

Quite contradictory opinions, aren't they? Which of them we should believe and follow? If I were you I'd naturally buy books from different lotto experts and put them into action to compare. Yet, like me, you would rather not spend even a dollar to buy a cat in the sack. I mean Ken Silver's **The Honest Lotto Link System**, as it was called at the time I was writing my eBay lotto manual and **Silver Lotto System**, as it was called later.

I criticized it in that manual saying that he denies scientific approach when he calls most systems *mathematical mumbo-jumbo* and at the same time he makes a steep turn presenting his system as a little known secret formula.

"A formula — by the way, the only one — does underlie all the systems but, dear Ken," polymerized I, "it is known to all the educated people who has read something about probability of descrite events like, at least, tossing a coin and its outcomes, and not a secret at all. I'll comment on it closely in about 20 pages from here. If you show me another formula, you are a lotto genius."

Spend As Little As $10 A Game To Get Results was his general statement. Of course, you can get some results, but what ones?

Surprisingly, but I ran into his site later again. He had updated it. I found more testimonials to attract a buyer. But what do they testify to?

The answer is:any lotto system can work all right and bring sometimes big wins when <u>thousands of people begin to employ it!</u> The difference is in the fact how much money you put into it. Those who put more, get more prizes.

But selling his system Ken made 2 rude mistakes in his advertising. Just ponder on this point:**Fill Out Tickets Only Once!** And then on this one:**Up To 98% Win Rating!**

For me, a lotto specialist with years of my own great lotto practice, filling out tickets only once means that you launch a set of selected numbers that you don't change through a group of draws and just wait and wait and wait until you win something in a few of them but not with up to 98% win rating and, besides, spending only, as Ken declares, "As Little As $10 A Game To Get Results"

I had to criticize even some Gale Horward's statements and the Australian guy's eBay materials, too. Tell me how to choose your own numbers in a certain draw by analyzing the sums of the numbers and discovering that more than 70% of the past sets of winning numbers are produced by only 27 or 28% of all the possible sums.

That is just lottery statistics and a player always wants to have certain winning numbers. This solid mathematical generalization is good for me, a person who has passed all the way from a green lotto novice to lotto professional, and who could reach the summit of lotto theory and then come back again to his lotto practice, enriched by his own class of wheels.

My criticism also refers to the Smart Play Zones from the System-X. They deal with the probable sets of numbers which are aimed for wheeling. However, each lottery player would like to know how to pick specific winning numbers for a certain draw.

This is what I have always focused my efforts on and now look at what I have achieved.

HOW I FIRST HIT 4 IN 5 IN OUR PICK 5 FROM 36 LOTTERY

In the autumn of 1984 I was a two-year student of the English Faculty of our local Teacher's Training Institute. I was 27 and in August my second daughter was born. So, I had to look for some extra ways of earning money. I was a bright student and the Institute paid me a monthly scholarship but it was not enough for the family of four. Soon I found an evening job in a food shop nearby.

One day someone, I don't remember who exactly, told me to try my luck with our State Lotteries 5 out of 36 and 6 out of 49. They had already been in progress in the USSR since 1970. I laughed him off and said what most of people usually say:"Never play gambling with your state!" But he intrigued me and once I found myself at a lottery kiosk and wrote down the results of the played draws and…three months later I won 4 in 5 winning numbers in a draw.

And by the beginning of 1985 I had already been in the habit of putting down the lotto results into some notepad and racking my brains over them.

It should be remarked that the results of any lottery are always presented from the last draw to the current one within a selected list of draws. Visually, from the bottom of the list to its top. **To start winning, you have to rewrite them into your pad upside down.**

Below are the tripled marked results of Pick 5 from 36 lottery from the beginning of 1985. And at that time they were drawn by a lotto machine with a horizontal mixing of the balls once a week.

	Just Periodicals	Distant Similarity	Pattern Shifts
Draw01	03-15-26-30-32	03-15-26-30-32	03-15-26-30-32
Draw02	10-**14**-24-28-32	10-14-24-28-32	10-14-24-28-32
Draw03	07-11-**14**-22-25	07-11-14-22-25	07-11-14-22-25
Draw04	**04**-05-**14**-22-24	04-05-14-22-24	04-05-14-22-24
Draw05	12-23-29-31-34	12-23-29-31-34	12-23-29-31-34
Draw06	**04**-08-15-27-31	04-08-15-27-31	04-08-15-27-31
Draw07	01-10-15-28-33	**01**-10-**15**-28-33	01-10-15-28-33
Draw08	**04**-08-20-30-32	**04**-**08**-20-30-32	04-08-20-30-32
Draw09	22-24-32-34-36	22-24-32-34-36	22-24-32-34-36
Draw10	14-19-25-29-33	14-19-25-29-33	**14**-**19**-**25**-29-33
Draw11	01-13-15-31-34	**01**-13-**15**-31-34	01-13-15-31-34
Draw12	04-08-13-19-36	**04**-**08**-13-19-36	04-**08**-**13**-**19**-36
Draw13	????????????????	????????????????	????????????????

Observing them and thinking over them I discovered periodical properties of that lottery process that can be traced through the winning numbers in the way you can see with number **14** in Draws 02,03,04 and with number **04** in Draws 04,06,08. They repeated themselves with different repeating intervals, zero and one correspondingly. Later I called the winning numbers with such behavior **periodicals.**

My attention was also attracted to Draws 07, 08 and 11, 12. In them a couple of numbers — **01**, **15** and **04**, **08** — followed one after another with a striking stability so that you could assume that some balls from 20-29 and 30-36 groups might appear in Draw13 because they poped up in Draw 09. But which of them exactly? Wait a bit and see below.

Those earliest observations convinced me — **periodicity was a "visit card" of our pioneer Lottotrons,** this is how a ball-stirring machine is called in Russia, and that I could attempt to rely on it in predicting the future outcomes.

I can still recall that at those days before Draw13 I was also absorbed in looking for *matching geometrical pattern shifts* of the balls. What do I mean?

Look at the whole 36-number playing field. Now they are arranged in the order they are settled on our lottery 5x36 tickets.

Pattern Shifts

Draw 10	Draw 12	(only 3 winning numbers from all the5)
01 07 13 **19 25** 31	01 07 **13 19** 25 31	
02 08 **14** 20 26 32	02 **08** 14 20 26 32	
03 09 15 21 27 33	03 09 15 21 27 33	

04 10 16 22 28 34   04 10 16 22 28 34
05 11 17 23 29 35   05 11 17 23 29 35
06 12 18 24 30 36   06 12 18 24 30 36

Now looking at the two columns you can clearly see that the winning numbers **08**, **13**, **19** in Draw 12 are the result of a left shift of the same three-number pattern **14**, **19**, **25** in Draw 10.

That prompted me to mark the numbers in Draw 09 and to connect them all to get the pattern they would produce. And what will you see if you do the same now? A silhouette of a chair in its profile!

Draw09

01	07	13	19	25	31
02	08	14	20	26	**32**
03	09	15	21	27	33
04	10	16	**22**	23	**34**
05	11	17	18	29	35
06	12	18	**24**	30	**36**

And what did I decide after that, taking into consideration all I have just told you above, especially my assumption of 20s and 30s groups?

I SIMPLY SHIFTED THE CHAIR...A STEP UPWARDS!!!

Draw13

01	07	13	19	25	**31**
02	08	14	20	26	32
03	09	15	**21**	27	**33**
04	10	16	22	28	34
05	11	17	**23**	29	**35**
06	12	18	24	30	36

```
      31

21  —  23

23     25
```

It proved to be the right extrapolation and after the balls had been drawn I saw the result. **Draw 13:** **06 – 21– 23 – 31– 33,** with 06 as the only one missing number.

Paying 30 kopeeks=cents for the variant I won 91 dollars (at that time our 1 rouble was approximately equal to 1 dollar), more than twice of my monthly student's allowance, but I was so sorry that I hadn't multiplied the winning combination of the numbers.

On the other hand, I was proud and happy a week later pushing our perambulator with my second daughter to a retailer's booth (a kiosk in Russian) to get the money and pondering over the **BEAUTY of CHANCE.**

At this place of the narration let me quote once more from one of the sources above:**"It would likely take many thousands, if not hundreds of thousands of draws to begin to see such trends".**

Well, my lotto brothers and sisters, it took me only 13 draws to watch the trend and to make use of it skillfully and in time. The POWER of OBSERVATION—that's all!

Matching pattern shifts helped me in that draw and further, in my mature practice. Today I am still using them when they, according to my predictions, may occur. And at that time it was just my intermediate stage on the path to my lotto peaks.

However, if you are used to drawing or embroidering (suppose you are an artist or a housewife) it may be better for you to watch the geometric patterns of all the winning numbers among your draws or part of them and give names to them and use the patterns in your lotto practice.

Thus, **any method of analysis founded on your precise observations is valid if afterwards it can be generalized and can lead you to your future wins**.

MY FIRST MATRIXES FOR PICK5 FROM 36 LOTTERY

Also, by that time I had already discovered the inner mechanism of constructing any representative of my own class of balanced AWMs and from time to time I was busy enlarging the number of them for wheeling up to one third of the numbers of a certain new lottery they introduced for us in Russia or I used to find in the other countries via the Internet after 2001 when it firmly came into my life.

So, at the end of 1985, after a year of playing, I could enumerate, at least, twenty draws in which I had predicted 3, 4 or even 5 WNs among my 8 to 15 SNs, but I could hardly place all of them on one playing 6x6 square field without, as I felt, some tricky mechanism of wheeling them.

That was a problem and I decided to try to solve it graphically as I was not a mathematician, though at the TIACSR for a semester they taught the students *The Basics of the Theory of Probability*.

I clearly remembered that main formula of combining m-members out of n-members, where m < n by 1 digit.

$$C_n^m = \frac{n \times (n-1)\ldots(n-(m-1))}{m \times (m-1)\ldots 3 \times 2 \times 1}$$

How to use it? It's very simple. Supposing you have selected 10 numbers out of the set of the numbers your specific national lottery comprises. And supposing your lottery is a Pick5/36.

In that case m =5, n =10 and your

$$C_n^m = (10 \times 9 \times 8 \times 7 \times 6){:}(5 \times 4 \times 3 \times 2 \times 1) = 252.$$

252 combinations and – the only one variant with 5 WNs! Is it reasonable to waste \$252 per a draw not knowing exactly whether some or all of your winning numbers are inside your chosen group or not?

So-called full systems (full wheels), which contain all the possible combinations that can be made up from a group of some selected numbers and which are often officially offered by lotto authorities on their sites, ads and lotto tickets **are based on the Formula** and, therefore, are very expensive if you want to wheel a large group of your selected numbers.

And mind! I would never call them systems either, but just wheels, which would be more correct. And even more precisely – Wheeling Matrixes, because when presented graphically with empty and occupied positions, with enumerated lines and columns, they really look like mathematic matrixes. What I wanted to get was the

Abbreviated Wheeling Matrix (AWM), which, encoded in a certain way, is an excerpt from the formula.

Such a matrix can be compared with a trap for multiple lotto wins when, at least, three or more of your winning numbers are within the group of your selected numbers wheeled by a matrix. And you can always calculate its guaranteed minimum.

And, indeed, after formulating the right mathematical task in my mind, I invented the encoding mechanism and in the first half of 1986 built the whole class of my AWMs graphically – from the narrowest, able to wheel only 7 numbers in 5x36 lottery, to the widest ones that could wheel half of all the numbers in a lottery.

And the most remarkable thing was that they were different from the rest of the matrixes I found in various lotto sources later being and looking, first of all, compact and convenient in lotto practice. In fact, all of them have always been a compressed graphical presentation of the above formula in which m=2 and n=7, 8, 9...up to half of the numbers drawn in a lottery.

So, I was proud of myself and full of positive emotions and expectations.

Their class starts with this smallest Pick 5 in 36 one with its 5 lines, in which 7 selected numbers can be wheeled.

•	•				•	•
	•		•	•		•
•		•	•		•	
•		•		•		•
	•	•		•	•	

If your selected numbers are 1-2-3-4-5-6-7, line 01 gives you the following 3 variants:

1-2-6-7 + 3 / 1-2-6-7 + 4 / 1-2-6-7 + 5

Line 02 gives you 2-4-5-7 + 1 / 2-4-5-7 + 3 / 2-4-5-7 + 6 and so on.

On the whole, you have 15 variants.

If, for example, the winning numbers are 01-03-05-06, then you have such multiple wins as:

In line 01 they are **1**-2-**6**-7 + **3** / 1-2-6-7 + 4 / **1**-2-**6**-7 + **5**

In line 02 there are no wins.

In line 03 they are **1**-**3**-4-**6** + 2 / **1**-**3**-4-**6** + **5** / **1**-**3**-4-**6** + 7

The AWM brings you your 4in5 win in line 03, and if you continue, in line 04 and 05.

HOW MOG WAS BORN AND BECAME MATURED

My UNIVERSAL METHORD of SELECTING WINNINING NUMBERS was born and then thoroughly developed after this 5 x36 **Unbelievable Draw 09**.

It was **January 1987** and I was lying in a hospital bed with Hepatitis A, which I had caught from one of my junior students at secondary school 33 where I was working temporaraly as a Technology teacher. Not waisting the time I was learning English Lexicology for one of my summer exams. Luckily, I took my lottery notes with me and I switched to them quite often for a change of mental activity and relaxing.

One day when I was looking through the list of results of some previous 5x36 draws from the beginning of 1986 and marking periodicals in them I ran into Draw 09 and...

It was a moment of enlightenment!

Draw03	**06**-11-**12**-13-18	06-11-12-13-18
Draw04	04-17-20-31-36	04-17-20-31-36
Draw05	05-16-**26**-30-31	05-16-26-30-31
Draw06	**06**-09-**12**-14-19	06-09-12-14-19
Draw07	**03**-06-08-**26**-32	03-06-08-26-32
Draw08	**03**-05-25-32-35	03-**05**-**25**-32-**35**
Draw09	**03**-**06**-**12**-15-**26**	03-06-**12**-**15**-26

Draw 09 was absolutely predictable!

Looking at the marked numbers you could predict beforehand, up to your last one, what 5 numbers were going to hit.

With **06** and **12** as "**X – – X – – X**" pattern periodicals.

With **26** as "**X – X – X**" pattern periodical.

With **03** as "**XXX**" pattern periodical.

And finally, with 15 as the lacking **L**ast **D**igit **N**umber (**LDN**) in the **05** – 15 – **25** – **35** succession.

"This type of a Lottotron with the horizontal mixing mechanism of the balls reveals regular periodicity in some popping up numbers," I concluded from the draw. "In that case <u>I CAN USE ITS PECULIARITY TO BET ON SOME REPEATING NUMBERS FOR THE THIRD TIME AND IF THE BALLS APPEAR, THEY ARE MINE</u>".

It was also from that draw that I put my trust into an **LDN**, as you can see with the succession 05-**15**-25-35 within numbers 01 to 36. What a prodigy! What a contradiction to the laws of chance!

Objectively, number 32 was another candidate for DRAW 09 according to its "**XXX**" pattern and number 04 or number 24 could equally hit being the descending 04 or 24 numbers in the "**06->05**->04-?" and "**26->25**->24-?" successions. So, to hit the jack pot you'd have to bet on a few variants minimizing them with the Draw 08 structure like these

04-06-12-26-32 / 04-06-12-24-32 /03-04-06-12-26 / 03-04-06-12-24 …

And in the end 03-**06**-**12**-15-**26**

The conclusion was obvious:SEPARATE NUMBERS AND EVEN COUPLES OF NUMBERS SOMETIMES GATHER TOGETHER IN A THIRD IN ORDER DRAW GIVING YOU A CHANCE TO PREDICT ALL THE HITTING NUMBERS OR MOST OF THEM OR SOME OF THEM, WHICH IS WONDERFUL IN ITSELF NEVERTHELESS.

Besides, **that unforgettable draw** led me to the idea of obligatory automatic wheeling my selected numbers 03-04-06-12-15-24-26-32 in some abbreviated matrix in order to exclude my inevitable subjective mistakes at combining them by hand. I remember lying on the hospital bed making up the biggest matrix in my life with its 36 numbers. It took me nearly a day to build it up and I was not sure that it was carefully balanced, namely, without excessive lines but it was a useful exercise.

Two weeks later I left the hospital with the KEY TO SUCCESS and nearly at once I seized the opportunity to confirm my method of selecting WNs=winning numbers.

1987 lotto year started with the following 5x36 results:

Draw01	**07**-25-28-30-**35**
Draw02	05-11-13-14-29
Draw03	04-11-16-20-21
Draw04	**07**-09-20-27-**35**
Draw05	01-**08**-13-31-33
Draw06	**08**-09-12-15-36
Draw07	???????????????????

Using my method of selecting I expected the hitting of **07**, **08**, **35** periodicals in Draw07. Looking at the structure of Draw06, I made an assumption that some certain balls from 10-19 group might add to them. Consecutive numbers 13-14 from Draw02 were enough for me at that time to add the teens to them in the following way: 10-11, 11-12, 12-13…17-18, 18-19, 19-10. The result of the draw was **08**-17-18-22-**35** and I won a second prize and two third prizes.

It was going to be fun and I decided to share my lotto experience with someone else.

So, that year by Draw45 I had already played in a lotto group of 3 including me. However, our 6 eyes missed that remarkable gathering of the winning balls you can see in the table of results below.

Draw39	**04**-13-15-**18**-35
Draw40	02-17-27-31-33
Draw41	06-07-14-22-**24**
Draw42	**04**-**18**-19-25-36
Draw43	02-18-21-**24**-28
Draw44	03-08-23-26-33
Draw45	**04**-**18**-**24**-26-27

I remember being even furious for some time because its jack pot, 10000rur, was practically in our hands. Looking at Draw 43 and 44 with their numbers from 20-29 group, it was highly probable that with **04, 18, 24** periodicals I would try 20-21, 21-22, …26-27…28-29 couples as above, in Draw 07 with 10..19 group!

That's why it was after that draw that for the first time I started insisting on our UNINTERRUPTED LOTTO OBSERVATION SERVICE.

WEDDING RING ADVENTURE

The apex of playing in the loto syndicate was Draw35 in 1988. It was the end of June and I just graduated from the Teachers' Training Institute and met the summer as an unemployed.

But Pick5 from 36 lottery couldn't wait for me too long revealing itself in Draws 29 to 34 after which I understood I had to act, as Draw 35 looked like extremely predictable and favorable.

Draw29	**04**-10-**15**-19-22
Draw30	08-12-19-28-32
Draw31	01-06-**07**-20-21
Draw32	**04**-12-**15**-23-26
Draw33	**07**-19-20-32-36
Draw34	02-05-13-20-32

So, I did the only thing possible for me. I pawned my wedding ring to buy lottery tickets. How many do you think? 100! Each ticket had two playing zones, hence I had 200 variants. That cost me $60, half the price of the ring.

The draw was a hard nut again, with **20** and **32** as its two "XXX" periodicals that could hit together (less probably) or either of them (more probably) though in the end neither of them didn't.

Feeling a big fish I filled out ticket after ticket using my AWMs of different size and made a lot of bets without AWMs.

On that Sunday morning, the day on which our weekly drawings were broadcast I, as part of my old traditional ceremony, put on my formal gray suit and a tie and bare-footed, I was watching the balls on TV poping up one after another and producing such an outcome:

Draw 35   **04**-06-**07**-**15**-27

The total amount of my win was $454, with 3 second prizes (4 in 5) and 44 third ones (3 in 5). I hit both number 06 and number 27, though, to my regret, not in one playing zone. And I used only half of the tickets, still doubting in what I had discovered in that deceiving display of random numbers.

Two other members of our lotto pool were away on business and I shared the victory with our next-door neighbor, Alexander, who I had persuaded to try his fortune explaining to him what was going to happen and my know-how just before the draw.

While I was counting my prizes, there was a loud knock on our front door and a few seconds later Alexander squeezed me in his arms with the happiest face, for he won $270 and that was his monthly income as an engineer. Now he has been living with his family in Vancouver, Canada, since 2000. Those were the moments of great emotions! It's worth playing in a pool to feel them again.

But that instructive and dramatic draw helped me OVERCOME MY DOUBTS IN MY METHOD AND MADE MYSELF BELIEVE ABSOLUTELY IN A SCIENTIFICALLY PRE-CALCULATED LUCKY CHANCE.

"Remember!" repeated I to myself, "the Law of the Third Hit is the Diamond of your MOG".

PRINCIPLE OF EQUALITY OF OUTCOMES OF YOUR SNS

As you can judge now by the above examples my method of selecting winning numbers can make wonders in the hands of a professional player. IT LIMITS YOUR CHOICES TO SOME SPECIFIC NUMBERS that might come out in the current draw after the latest one.

But before the EVENT has taken place YOU CAN ONLY ASSUME THAT ONLY SOME OF THEM WILL BE WINNING. Surely, your rich past lotto experience, your sharpened lotto skills and your intuition can help you make your preferences with better chances.

The unchanged can be only the following. **Due to some inner periodical nature of your mixing machines and, as I have found much later, on the contrary to it, you are expecting that some of your selected numbers are likely to appear on the third time after their first and second apperance and gather together in the current draw which becomes their third one.**

Today the situation is evidentally worse for predicting winning numbers. The design of lotto machines has been changed greatly for the past fifty years. I think their manufactures couldn't help noticing that periodicity with which some winning numbers would come out. So they ordered that their lottotrons demonstrate more random distribution of outcomes. We know that today even a set of balls can be replaced for an every draw like it happens in the UK.

Fortunately, despite all the changes my MOG works and now let's see its component parts.

METHOD OF GATHERING FULL-SCALE DESCRIPTION

In fact, my method of selecting winning numbers is my developed detailed elaboration of the Gail Horward's statement I've already quoted above: *"Lottery numbers are randomly drawn. But randomly drawn numbers form patterns that are to a certain extent predictable"*.

MOG is a scientific method of picking winning numbers. It is based on Objectively Observed Anomalies (OOA), which I discovered, traced back, successfully used and is still employing in different types of lotteries. OOA, in their turn, are founded on three inner properties – Periodicity, Supplementation and Correlation – revealed in a number of distributions drawn by either a real Lottotron or, believe it or not, a random number generator (RNG), which is now employed in most of our online lotteries.

AND THE FACT THAT **MOG** BRILLIANTLY WORKS UNDER SUCH UNFAVORABLE CIRCUMSTANCES IS THE MOST AWESOME ONE THAT MAKES MY METHOD PERFECT AND UNIVERSAL! MOG with its set of rules is such an original method of selecting WNs that, like our fingerprints, it is unique and one of a few objective methods in this zone of entertainment.

MOG is a hierarchy of a dozen GOLDEN, SILVER, BRONZE, and IRON rules of picking numbers for every new draw using at least 10 or more, but not too many, results of past draws.

Note that each rule is illustrated with 2006-year examples from various world lotteries. I decided not to update the examples because from a year to a year they are just the same.

The Law of the Third Hit is the essence of nearly all the rules!

GOLDEN RULE #1

If a number repeats itself twice with Period 0, Period 1 (over 1 draw), Period 2 (over 2 draws) or Period 3 (over 3 draws) – bet on it for the third time and if it pops out it is yours! Sometimes a couple of numbers can demonstrate such an outcome and sometimes, as it can often be observed in our Keno, Joker, Rapido and Top3 a number hits again and again and appears 4, 5 and even more times with different periodical HM (hitting-missing) patterns.

PERIOD 0, (P0) or XXX pattern

The USA, state
Washington, 6 in 49:   **03**-12-18-28-43-47
                        03-10-13-15-18-35

03-05-11-16-20-37
03-19-42-44-46-49

The UK, 6 in 49 + bonus
(not included):

06-21-28-34-**38**-41

06-19-22-**38**-39-43
24-**38**-40-44-47-48

Australia,
Oz lotto + 2 bonuses
(not included):

07-15-**16**-33-38-43

06-12-**16**-17-32-35
16-25-28-32-34-36

The Russian Federation,
Keno 7 in 56:

02-05-**12**-31-35-49-55

06-**12**-29-30-35-42-47
10-**12**-14-20-29-41-42
10-**12**-17-33-35-37-56

PERIOD 1, (P1) or X-X-X pattern

The USA, state
Washington, 6 in 49:

24-36-38-39-**44**-48
09-15-16-18-24-30
04-21-24-27-**44**-47
01-11-23-39-40-41
01-05-18-43-**44**-48
01-15-17-30-37-47
06-16-22-33-40-**44**

The UK, 6 in 49 + bonus
(not included):

06-**19**-22-38-39-43

24-38-40-44-47-48
17-**19**-20-35-43-45
11-14-17-34-37-43
01-10-11-18-**19**-46

Australia, Oz lotto + 2 bonuses: 04-08-12-13-29-44 +<u>19</u>-**23**
04-13-21-33-42-43 +14-<u>19</u>
11-15-<u>19</u>-**23**-37-41 +01-08
11-14-15-18-27-30 +06-39
05-12-14-**23**-36-39 +16-22

The Russian Federation, 6 in 45: 05-18-25-**29**-31-32
07-12-13-23-34-37
12-17-25-**29**-34-42
09-16-24-26-27-36
05-09-10-13-**29**-44

<u>PERIOD 2</u>, (P2) or X - - X - - X pattern

Canada, 6 in 49 + bonus   03-14-**26-27**-35-44
(not included):

04-10-14-19-21-28
01-05-12-17-31-44
21-22-**26-27**-40-47
04-05-26-33-38-44
01-09-25-27-37-40
03-15-17-**26-27**-46

The USA, state   06-08-13-**18**-24-42
Washington, 6 in 49:

08-11-22-31-36-44
07-10-18-26-30-43
11-14-**18**-20-30-36
03-08-11-28-42-48
07-15-25-35-38-44
03-12-**18**-28-43-47

Australia, Oz lotto + 2 bonuses:	**09**-10-**23**-40-41-42 +06-14
	06-17-21-25-26-37 +07-16
	02-08-16-19-22-34 +14-40
	09-11-12-**23**-24-39 +31-44
	01-21-29-32-33-45 +02-31
	13-21-26-29-32-45 +06-25
	09-10-13-**23**-26-42 +07-33

The Russian Federation, 6 in 49:	10-11-**17**-24-36-48
	05-08-37-43-47-48
	01-07-09-22-32-43
	03-15-**17**-25-38-39
	02-04-16-30-44-49
	08-19-25-27-28-45
	17-20-23-30-42-45

It's a special pattern and was my favorite one for many years because it can be presented by 2 WNs

PERIOD 3, (P3) or or X - - - X - - - X pattern

The USA, state Washington, 6 in 49:	23-**27**-32-39-47-48
	03-06-12-38-44-47

                               03-10-27-28-29-36
                               01-05-19-37-38-39
                               18-24-**27**-30-31-33
                               15-20-32-35-37-42
                               06-12-23-35-41-49
                               06-13-26-35-36-48
                               03-07-**27**-30-37-48

The Russian Federation, 6 in 49:   **11**-12-30-36-43-47
                               03-07-28-29-34-41
                               08-16-26-37-41-42
                               03-10-19-23-24-42
                               01-**11**-12-21-34-42
                               01-02-09-12-13-24
                               05-14-15-32-38-41
                               12-15-23-26-29-31
                               10-**11**-17-24-36-48

PERIOD 3 is observed more rarely but I used to rely on it
and win, so I wouldn't neglect it if structurally you feel it
may occur.

GOLDEN RULE #2

I call it BROKEN PERIODICALS (BPs) **and it's better
to illustrate it than to describe in words. It is also based
on hitting of one and the same number three, four and
more times.**

Look in what patterns it can reveal itself:

X	X	X	X	X
X	(missed)	X	X	(missed)
(missed)	X	X	(missed)	X
X	X	(missed)	X	X
		X	X	X

Euro Million (only red balls):   14-18-19-31-**37**
04-07-33-**37**-39
15-24-28-44-47
33-36-**37**-42-45

Euro Million (only red balls):   06-10-**21**-45-49
05-06-16-23-27
15-16-**21**-36-38
01-03-**21**-32-39

Canada, 6 in 49 + bonus: 01-**02**-07-16-43-44+20
12-17-25-26-43-44+**02**
02-17-35-41-46-48+05
09-27-32-38-39-49+46
02-23-25-33-34-41+03

The UK, 6 in 49 + bonus: 01-**03**-22-32-38-44+45
03-21-31-42-47-48+34
07-19-20-29-41-49+18
01-**03**-04-05-17-37+30
01-**03**-26-34-43-47+12

The Russian Federation, 6 in 49:   02-04-15-30-37-**42**
                                      06-07-23-26-37-47
                                      06-15-21-24-27-**42**
                                      04-16-33-36-37-**42**
                                      09-18-36-37-38-**42**

In the year when I was writing my eBay Lotto Manual, in the UK National Lottery you could watch it appear twice, **irrespective of the ball sets and lotto machines that were changed at random!** Just have a look at its another variant as X-m-XX-m-X pattern:

879	11-15-18-24-34-**44** +28
880	01-04-06-18-19-40 +30
881	05-22-26-40-42-43 +**44**
883	05-08-09-26-29-**44** +16
884	01-12-23-26-35-45 +43
885	07-22-35-**44**-48-49 +16

(as you can make sure, it even works with a bonus ball!)

890	**06**-08-21-25-43-47 +16
891	05-10-11-16-17-33 +13
892	**06**-09-31-32-40-47 +24
893	**06**-27-33-38-45-47 +08
894	01-03-11-16-23-36 +22
895	**06**-09-13-15-40-43 +02

Sometimes a number can repeat itself 5 or more times with a broken period, draw after draw, and you should decide whether to keep on betting on it after the third time or not. **I recommend betting because if it is drawn again, it is yours.**

US, state WA, lotto 6 in	49:**03**-08-11-28-42-48
	07-15-25-35-38-44
	03-12-18-28-43-47
	03-10-13-15-18-35
	03-05-11-16-20-37
	03-19-42-44-46-49
	01-06-10-13-43-45
	03-14-15-17-19-32

Russia, lotto 6 in 45:	03-26-30-41-**42**-44
	05-06-08-29-40-**42**
	02-05-23-34-**42**-44
	01-04-27-31-33-43
	07-15-19-31-**42**-45
	03-14-21-28-32-**42**

GOLDEN RULE #3

It demonstrates close descending +/- 1 correlation observed in any three or more than three draws following one another. **If in a couple of adjacent draws there are two numbers, which are different from each other in one digit, then in the next draw after them you should bet on the number that is either less or more in a one comparing to the number in the middle draw.**

Euro Million (only red balls):	**02**-23-28-40-43
	03-21-30-34-35
	04-23-24-28-34

UK lotto, 6 in 49 w/o bonus:	05-22-26-40-42-**43**
	05-08-09-26-29-**44**
	01-12-23-26-35-**45**
Canada, 6 in 49 w/o bonus:	21-22-26-**27**-40-47
	04-05-**26**-33-38-44
	01-09-**25**-27-37-40

June 2013, Russian 2 to 10 in 20 from 80 Keno:

05.06	04,09,10,12,14,15,17,20,21,25,**28**,34,41,53,59,62,68, 70,74,78
06.06	02,03,08,10,11,20,**27**,28,31,39,41,43,45,47,50,53,57,6 0,65,71
07.06	01,03,05,08,14,21,**26**,27,34,39,40,43,49,51,61,63,68, 71,73,80
08.06	07,17,20,**25**,26,29,30,31,32,34,39,45,47,48,49,50,54, 58,74,77
09.06	01,04,07,10,21,**24**,28,30,37,38,39,40,45,48,57,61,63, 67,70,76
10.06	04,11,18,**23**,25,26,29,30,32,35,42,51,55,58,59,64,67, 70,78,79

The most terrific thing here is that they are not drawn by a real lotto machine, but by a random numbers generator. My MOG beats it, too, like many years ago when it beat real lottotrons. Sometimes at the sight of that I go into rapture. AND IT MEANS THAT YOU CAN BEAT YOURS, TOO.

SILVER RULE #1

It is based on the principle of supplementation within two successive draws. **It deals with a supplementing number or 2 of them inside a couple of numbers. Or outside them, with a left or right supplementing number or sometimes both like in my last example.**

| Canada, 6 in 49 w/o bonus (one gap number between): | 09-**12**-**14**-19-31-43 |
| | 11-**13**-18-20-24-29 |

| US, state WA, 6 in 49 (two gap numbers between): | 05-11-12-**15**-**18**-26 |
| | 08-**16**-**17**-20-32-40 |

| Russian 7 in 56 (an adjacent number on the left): | 18-26-27-35-**51**-**52**-54 |
| | 17-21-23-35-41-**50**-55 |

| Australian Oz Lotto (an adjacent number on the right): | 15-22-**30**-**31**-34-41 |
| | 03-15-16-23-**32**-36 |

| Russian 6 in 45 (both adjacent left-right numbers): | 01-13-**22**-**23**-31-43 |
| | 03-17-**21**-**24**-39-40 |

SILVER RULE #2

If in a group of any two draws you see a couple of numbers with +/- 10 difference between them, then in your third draw you should bet on the last digit number, which is the highest or the lowest among three of them when put in a line; and if it pops out – it is yours.

UK, 6 in 49 w/o bonus:	06-27-**33**-38-45-47
	01-03-11-16-**23**-36
	06-09-**13**-15-40-43

Canada, 6 in 49 w/o bonus:	03-17-22-25-**40**-46
	01-10-18-20-**30**-40
	20-33-36-45-46-47

Australian Oz lotto +2 bonuses:	11-14-15-18-27-30+**06**-39
	05-12-14-23-36-39+**16**-22
	04-13-21-22-38-45+11-**26**

Russian lotto 6 in 45:	**07**-15-19-20-24-36
	02-06-**17**-20-23-34
	01-15-18-25-**27**-44

US, state WA, Pick 6 in 49:	03-08-11-28-42-**48**
	07-15-25-35-**38**-44
	03-12-18-**28**-43-47
	03-10-13-15-**18**-35

Russian Pick 6 in 49 lottery:	**17**-20-23-30-42-45
	03-08-12-**27**-29-31
	02-04-15-30-**37**-42
	06-07-23-26-37-**47**

SILVER RULE #3

If in a previous draw you can see a group of last digit numbers, consisting of two or more members, which, if

put one by one, are part of some progression, then in the next draw bet on the missing member/members of the progression and – it is/they are yours if it/they come out.

There is some lotto variety here, as you can make sure looking at the examples below. But the rule works and helps a lot at selecting your winning numbers.

UK lotto 6 in 49 w/o bonus:	01-**04**-05-25-**34**-46
	11-15-18-**24**-**34**-**44**
Euro Million (only red balls):	05-**06**-**16**-23-27
	15-**16**-21-**36**-38
Russian lotto 6 in 45:	06-**07**-23-26-**37**-**47**
	06-15-21-24-**27**-42
UK lotto 6 in 49 w/o bonus:(an ideal complementation!):	01-05-**08**-**18**-42-**48**
	06-21-**28**-34-**38**-41
Canada, 6 in 49, w/o bonus:	**05**-**15**-19-24-26-46
	07-19-31-43-**45**-49

Australian Oz lotto, w/o 2 bonuses:

(With these draws, we are witnesses of a unique supplementation):

09-21-**24**-31-**34**-43	09-**21**-24-**31**-34-43
08-11-**14**-26-41-**44**	08-**11**-14-26-**41**-44

As you can conclude from above examples, the diversity of similar outcomes is amazingly kaleidoscopic. This rule can be quite frequently applied to the results of your past draws and it becomes a pearl of your private lotto collection like above with 08-18-**28**-**38**-48, where the last digit progression is represented by all its members.

BRONZE RULE #1

If in any past draw you have two or three odd/even numbers from one of a group:01…09/10…19/20…29, etc.; then in you next draw try your luck with either missing members or, which is better, all of them because any couple ot triple of them can hit again.

These occur less frequently than the winning numbers selected by the golden and silver rules, yet you can bet on them if you use wheels to process properly all your selected numbers for a new draw.

Euro Million (only red balls):	14-18-19-**31**-**37**
	04-07-**33**-**37**-**39**
UK, 6 in 49 w/o bonus:	25-**30**-**34**-39-40-47
	01-03-22-**32**-**38**-44
Canada, 6 in 49 w/o bonus:	08-21-**24**-**26**-34-38
	05-13-16-**20**-**28**-31
Russian lotto 6 in 45:	08-19-**23**-**29**-31-33
	08-11-20-**21**-**27**-44

As you can see from the examples above, not all the members from these odd/even progressions can come out. It is natural for a game of chance and, once more, if you use wheels your task is to wheel all the members of a progression with your other selected numbers, not to miss some of them in the progression.

BRONZE RULE #2

It can be called LONG-DISTANT REPETITION. **It is when observing some lotto results you discover that a few numbers from a previous group of adjacent draws in some part of a table of results begin to coincide with some numbers of a few last draws like in these examples.**

Canadian lottery, 6
in 49 +bonus:

January
01-**07**-26-40-**43-45** +46
03-08-**17**-20-26-47 +38
03-14-20-23-**25**-45 +12
01-20-23-36-38-49 +07
(…after 15 draws…)
March-April
07-19-31-**43**-**45**-49 +36
02-**03**-**17**-18-19-46 +30
03-17-22-**25**-40-46 +27
01-10-17-**20**-30-40 +34

In that case in your current draw you can simply try all the numbers of the second, third and fourth draw in the previous group as your newly selected numbers and, surely, some of them will be yours.

And here is another unique coincidence of 5 balls in the third successive draw that once occurred in

Australian Oz Lotto + 2 bonuses:

03-**12**-13-**23**-29-30 +18-37

07-16-**21**-25-**26**-**38** +24-43

07-**12**-22-**26**-**32**-37 +24-**33**

(…after 10 draws…)

05-**12**-14-**23**-36-39 +16-22

04-13-**21**-22-**38**-45 +11-**26**

07-11-**12**-20-25-**32** +**26**-**33**

Therefore, you should be always in a state of alert not to miss such lotto gems and the necessity to have your CONSTANT LOTTO OBSERVATION SERVICE **arises again.**

IRON ORIENTATING RULE.

When using the golden, silver and bronze rules, pay attention to the structure of the last draw to narrow your winning numbers search. By the structure of the last draw I mean which groups of tens (01…09/10…19/20…29/ etc.) are present in it.

As a rule, you can observe two types of structures both in a previous and a next draw:Correlated Structure (CS), when twenties hit after twenties and, saying, forties after forties; and Shifted Structure (SS) when previous WNs and followig WNs are from different groups.

Obviously, CS is much more predictable than SS and, luckily for us, it reveals quite often.

Hence, this rule is your supplementary means of selecting a group, two groups or more, in which your winning numbers can appear. And then you can apply to the groups all the other rules.

The examples are only a few below but quite enough to demonstrate the approach.

| US, state WA, 6 in 49, **CS**: | 19-21-31-37 -45-49 |
| | 13-26-28-31-44-47 |

| Euro Million (only red balls), **CS**: | 06-11-35-41-44 |
| | 09-13-34-41-42 |

| UK, 6 in 49 w/o bonus, **CS**: | 05-22-26-40-42-43 |
| 05-08-09-26-29-44 | |

| Russian lotto 7 in 56, **SS**: | *26*-*39*-45-48-**51-53-56** |
| | **06-08-10**-*12-14*-*32*-49 |

DESCENDING STEEP NUMBERS (DSN)

as X–(X+1)–(X+2) **or** X–(X-1)–(X-2) **patterns.**

This is an additional method of selecting only one winning number. It is another illustration of *the Law of the Third Hit*. **It works well with less predictable lotteries when you are at a loss what to select but you can discover them if you use the PROG with its extended presentation of outcomes.**

It is similar to Golden Rule #4 but with 2 gaps between three successive numbers.

As an example of this quite rare but remarkable development I copied some cut PROG zone.

File	D/T_hits	F+/-1	F_LDN	F+/-10	F_O/E	FS	Help!
10440				09 10	14		
10441			08		12 13		20
10442		06			14		21
10443		05		11			
10444	04		08			16	
10445		05 06					
10446	01						
10447		05	07 08	11		16	
10448	02		07				21

Lottery coincidence search (c) by MNK Oct 2009

In Draws 10443, 10445 and 10447 our DSNs are 05, 06 and 07 correspondingly. Draw 10447 is wonderful because MOG provides you with 3 WNs in it. They are:

05, with its X-X-X pattern
07, as the bottom member of its DSN group
08, with its X - - X - - X pattern

By the way, these are the freshest two-day summer 2019 results of our 5x36 lottery.

WHAT-AFTER-WHAT CORRELATIVE GROUP SELECTION AND NON-PERIODIC REPEATING COUPLES.

Again, these are the other additional methods of selecting either one winning number or a couple of them for less

predictable lotteries. And you need the PROG once more to notice such numbers on a playing area.

Below is a bigger table with a few what-after-what marked WNs from our Pick 5 in 36 lottery results of May 2010. Unlike today when we have 6 draws a day, it was played only once a day at that year.

You can see that 03 hit after 02 and 05 hit after 07 three times inside 01-09 group, 12 hit after 10 inside 10-19 group thrice too, as well as 20 after 22 in 20-29 group.

However, 14 hit after 16 only two times, being a cold number, the one who pops up rarely.

02 with 07 and 07 with 08 are just non-periodic couples which hit frequently but irregularly.

Surprisingly, but they produced the greatest part of SUPERGATHERING on May 23, 2010.

02 came out submitting to XXX pattern. 07 demonstrated X-XX broken period. 08 attached to 07

after their joined appearing on May 11, 16 and 20 with a propotionally lessening interval between the draws. 03 and 20 completed the whole picture of that UNIQUE DRAW with all the five easily predicted thanks to MOG winning numbers.

What a pity it happened at the end of that school year when I wasn't ready yet to draw my closer attention to the lottery.

File   D/T_hits   F+/-1   F_LDN   F+/-10   F_O/E   FS   Help!

File									
205	01		08				18		
305	02	05		10			17		
405	02			12		16 17			23
505				11 12				22	
605	03	05 07							
705		05	08	10					
805			08	12					22
905	01	06					20		
1005			09		13				23
1105	02		07 08						
1205							18	20	
1305	02		07						
1405	03	05		10			20	22	
1505					13	16			
1605		07 08			14		18		
1705			09				18		22
1805	03	06					20	22	
1905			08 09					22	
2005			07 08						
2105	02 04			11					
2205	02		07	11			18	22	
2305	02 03		07 08				20		
2405		05	08			16		22	
2505	02			10	14				
2605	03			12				22	

Thus, this method of selection in the company of non-periodic couples shows a good stability of repetition and can be definitely relied on!

ODD-EVEN LEFT-RIGHT DESCENDING
3-/4-MEMBER STEPS.

This is another awarding trick of selecting only one winning number. It also contributes to *the Law of the Third Hit*. Such outcomes are often observed inside

01-09/10-19/20-29…groups. The steps are based on such odd-even progressions as 01, 03, 05…or 02, 04, 06.

In June 2013 in our KENO, for example, we had two odd slides in 50s and 60s groups.

0206	02,03,07,13,16,20,21,22,45,46,47,5 0,51,58,**59**,63,70,71,72,75	**59**
0306	01,04,05,11,19,21,25,27,29,32,33,4 8,49,55,**57**,61,62,63,65,72	**57**
0406	01,10,11,12,16,21,22,24,25,31,36,4 8,**55**,57,60,66,67,75,76,78	**55**
0506	04,09,10,12,14,15,17,20,21,25,28,3 4,41,**53**,59,62,68,70,74,78	**53**
2006	06,07,10,15,18,26,27,28,29,30,48,5 3,59,**61**,65,71,72,74,76,77	**61**
2106	04,12,14,16,18,31,32,34,39,54,57,5 8,62,**63**,66,68,71,74,77,78	**63**
2206	03,04,05,12,13,18,19,28,29,36,42,4 6,48,52,55,57,63,**65**,66,68	**65**
2306	05,08,12,18,21,28,35,36,42,43,44, 45,50,60,61,63,65,**67**,72,80	**67**

There are 3 wonderful even left-right descending steps—24>26>**28**; 28>26>**24**; 32>30>28>**26**—on the PROG field at the beginning of June 5x36 lottery results in the same 2010.

Above them, at the end of May, we can see that WNs concentrate their hitting within 26, 27, 28 outcomes. And at last, on June 05, they present a lotto player with 5 WNs again. 29 hits as DSN 27 – 28 – 29 patten number and 31 what-after-what correlative one after 35, though 10 and 16 WNs in 04 June draw worsened your Pick 5 winning chances.

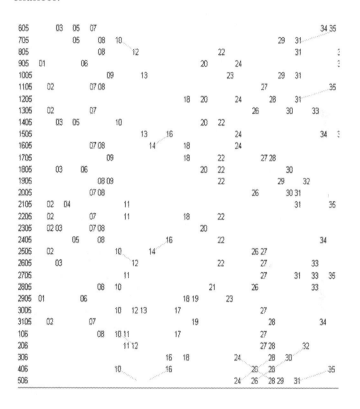

SOMETHING MORE IMPORTANT
ABOUT MATRIXES

Since the earliest time I invented my own AWMs for Pick 5
in 36 and Pick 6 in 49 lotteries which you can see below as
the stencils, where 5 left AWMs are for Pick 6 in49 lottery
and 2 right AWMs are for 5x36 one,

I have been still creating them when a new lottery is
introduced or when they make cheaper their lottery tickets

and it means that I can use longer AWMs and wheel more selected numbers.

There was some time in the late 1980s when I even wanted to patent them because the Central Lottery Office in Moscow, the capital of Russia, had issued their thin paperback lotto manual where I found a few AWMs different from mine. The authors of the booklet incorrectly called their matrixes systems. You know that to patent a new invention you have to compare it with a prototype. I found one for Pick6 from49 lottery in that booklet but no matter how hard I tried I couldn't understand how it was encoded and I gave up. Structurely, my variant of AWMs was with 4 or 5 fixed positions in a line of a matrix and the rest of the positions, one by one, added to the fixed ones providing you with 5- or 6-numer bets as in my example at the end of the chapter MY FIRST MATRIXES FOR Pick5 from 36 LOTTERY.

That prototype had 6 fixed numbers in each of its 22 lines and could wheel 12 selected numbers and bring you 3 from 6 WNs twice, as its guaranteed minimum, if they were among the 12 numbers.

Here it is in its inner perfect order, in which every member in the matrix representing a SN is repeated 11 times in every column.

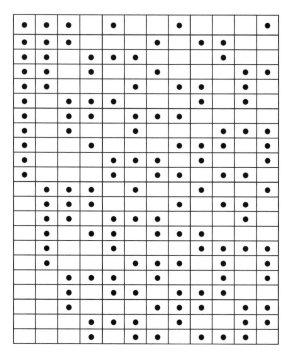

Quite often, on lots of sites, AWMs are presented in the letters of the alphabit. It's not visual, in my opinion. I always changed them into this sort of AWMs if I was interested in some of them.

Besides mine, I descovered and taught myself to construct two other classes of AWMs. One of them with 12 lines, for a Pick 5 lottery, was in the same old brochure. It generates WNs rather well if there are at least three of them among your selected ones. The peculiarity of the matrix is that in the first three columns a selected number is repeated 6 times while in the rest of them it is repeated 7 times.

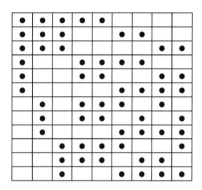

Mind that this spotted way of presentation gives you an opportunity to make the maximum use of it, placing your most promising SNs in the positions where they will be wheeled more frequently with the other SNs. The matrixes in their booklet prompted me to construct my own ones with only fixed positions of wheeled SNs in each line.

The other class of matrixes that I understood and learnt to construct I found in FREE 1000WEEKSLOTTO e-book that I mentioned as one of the lotto sources of my critical comments.

Presented graphically for 10 selected numbers for a Pick 6 lottery, it looked like this.

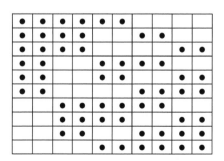

This is the easiest class to build up your similar AWMs by yourself.

In fact, it is a doubled realization the earlier mentioned formula when m=3 and n=more than 5.

In case n=5 you will get the following pre-matrix graphically like this one. In 10 lines it presents all the combinations of your selected numbers by three in a line.

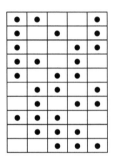

Then, double each position vertically and you will have the above Pick 6 in 10 AWM, though I changed the lines so that it could look more symmetrical.

Chronologically, I had to build my new AWMs for Keno when I first find it among Ukrainian online lotteries. I played them between 2005 and 2008 until Russian online lotteries appeared and I switched to them again. The years between 1998 and 2005 were the worst for the Russian lotteries when even the only offline lotto booth in the place where I lived was closed and I played lotteries occasionally having to get to a downtown booth which was too far away.

Downloading the Ukranian Keno database into the PROG and analizing its monthly results I descovered that Keno was the most predictable of the lotteries I had played before. The Ukrainian Keno formular was 2 to 10 in 20 WNs from 80. The Canadian Keno formular was 10 numbers shorter and I envied Derek and in 2010 found the Keno lottery with 62 numbers. People played it in Latvia, a small republic in northeastern Europe on the eastern coast of the Baltic Sea. It was one of the former Soviet Union Republics. I couldn't register in it being an outsider. So, I found a lotto player who had such an access and we played in a pool for a year and a half.

In short, this cluster of my Keno AWMs appeared after that events and every matrix of the group I tried at least once in a draw.

Below you can look at three of them, with their 10 fixed positions for your 10 selected numbers inside 16, 18 or 20 SNs to be wheeled through. They are exactly for 10 SNs per a bet because it enables you to have economical and at the same time effective wheeling tools.

Keno AWM for 16 SNs:

•	•	•	•	•							•	•	•	•	•
•	•				•	•	•	•	•	•				•	•
		•	•		•	•	•	•	•	•		•	•		
	•			•	•	•	•	•	•	•	•			•	

Keno AWM for 18 SNs:

1	2	3	4	5	6	7	8	9	10	11	12	13	14	15	16	17	18
•	•	•	•	•									•	•	•	•	•
•	•	•			•	•					•	•			•	•	•
•	•					•	•	•	•	•	•					•	•
		•	•		•	•	•			•	•	•		•	•		
	•		•	•	•			•	•		•	•	•		•		
•			•	•			•	•	•	•			•	•			•

Keno AWM for 20 SNs:

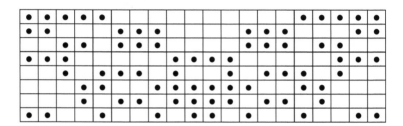

1	2	3	4	5	6	7	8	9	10	11	12	13	14	15	16	17	18	19	20
•	•	•	•	•											•	•	•	•	•
•	•				•	•	•					•	•	•				•	•
		•	•		•	•	•					•	•	•		•	•		
•	•	•						•	•	•	•						•	•	•
		•		•	•	•				•		•	•	•		•			
		•	•				•	•	•	•	•	•			•	•			
		•		•	•			•	•	•	•		•	•		•			
•	•			•			•			•	•				•			•	•

Let me remark that this last AWM is already balanced without Line 08. I added it later in order to have each of the twenty wheeling SNs repeated 4 times. You can agree that the eighth bet after the seventh first ones can be the bet that may bring you 10 in 10 prize too, provided that your 10 WNs are in the fixed positions of the eighth line or it can may enrich you in 5 in 10/6 in10/7 in 10, etc.

My latest AWMs that I constructed in the summer of 2018 and this summer of 2019 were for our JOKER lottery. It is a comparatively new lottery and for half a year I didn't pay attention at its results because a pack of cards has never been among my preferances to kill time.

Imagine what a nasty shock I had when I discovered that it was compiled of 52 cards and each card had its ordinal number different from its card value. It meant that it was a lottery consisting of 52 members and it turned out that the rules of the lottery resembled Keno rules, with its 9 WNs among 15 WNs drawn from 52.

What could be better for Keno-like games! So, I began to construct Joker AWMs enthusiastically.

Joker AWM for 13 SNs:

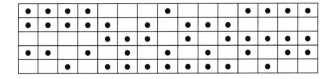

Joker AWM for 15 SNs:

On the pedestal in the PART 1& PART 2 pictures you can see the similar Joker AWM for 15 SNs.

It was my first variant of it but, unlike this one, it had unequel amount of fixed members of the matrix in each column, which are three now, though it looked beautiful and symmetrical with the piramid in the middle of the matrix.. It was balanced too, but it required a preliminary distribution of your SNs before wheeling them in the matrix, with your placing of the most probable SN in the middle position where it could be repeated 5 times.

In the summer of 2018 when there was a 15-minute interval between two draws I didn't have enough time for redistribution of my SNs, so I made up my mind to create the above matrix..

And here is the latest Joker AWM for 17 SNs which I constructed on July 15, 2019 between 3 pm and 4 pm during the second attempt. The first attempt was on August 22, 2018 between 7 and 8 pm when I created an assymetrical matrix with 7 lines and a central member which was repeated 7 times unlike its left and right neighbors with their 3 or 4 times.

And I was pleasantly surprised that a new variant of the matrix had only 6 lines being optimised and balanced perfectly. Another remarkable thing was that the matrix appeared balanced even without its 01-17 members in Line 06. I could add them to any of the 02 -16, 03-15, 04-14 or 05-13 positions.

Joker AWM for 17 SNs:

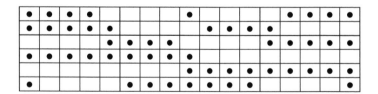

Mind that 17 numbers is practically one third of all the 52 numbers in the lottery. You don't need a wider matrix as my lotto practice shows me, though out of pure curiosity and

not to forget how I have always done it, I then constructed AWMs for 19 and 21 SNs.

Now you know with what tools I've been processing my SNs but the hardest task of a player is to fill a matrix with as many WNs among your SNs as possible. MOG is the only key to such filling but MOG without PROG is so a tiresome and time consuming lotto activity, especially when draws nearly come one after another, that this situation can easily turn you away from a lottery in which, in fact, you could become a millionaire in terms of your currency. But before coming to PROG and demonstrate and tell you how to use it I decided to include into the book this chapter from my eBay manual.

AROUND THE WORLD
LOTTO HUNT...

When in the summer of 2001 the Internet came into my life I got interested in the other countries national lotteries. By that time our best next-door neighbors—Alexander, his wife Galina and their two sons, qualified mogul skiers—had moved to Canada, so I started with the results of the British Columbia Canadian lottery. And I was not surprised at all when I had found that my MOG also worked nicely with it.

So in 2006, while writing my eBay lotto manual, I copied and filed a lot of fresh results from English, American, Canadian, Australian and European lotteries. I wanted to find out if my MOG was also applicable to them. So now let's get down to a bit of lotto hunting.

...IN CANADA.

Canadian lotto fans and players had a wonderful chance in their last Saturday draw in February 2004 in Lotto Pick6+bonus/49.

11 Sat	**03**-14-**26**-**27**-35-44+28		
12 Wen	04-10-14-19-21-28+12		
13 Sat	01-05-12-17-31-44+36		
14 Wen	21-22-**26**-**27**-40-47+**03**	26	27
15 Sat	04-05-26-33-38-**44**+49	26	
16 Wen	01-09-25-27-37-40+**45**	27	
17 Sat	**03**-15-17-**26**-**27**-**46** +38	**26**	**27**

You can see from above that the four winning numbers **03**, **26**, **27**, **46** could be easily predicted with my Golden Rules #1 and #4. The winning numbers **15**, **17** are among 05-**15**-35 and 07-**17**-47 according to Silver Rule#2. It is interesting to remark that the winning numbers **26** and **27** have, so to say, **double weight!!!**

Also, in Canada, in Ottawa, I found a wonderful lottery player, Derek by name, a retired architect and a high jumper in his youth, with his own lottery system, which he called APS (Anomaly Pattern System). Actually, he was the first to write to me on my eBay email enquiring about my Lotto Manual that I was selling at that time. Word by word and a couple of weeks later we became good friends and we are still now. He simply gained my favor when in one of his emails he told me whose photos he was keeping in his wallet in the 1960s. They were the pictures of his idols and both of them were Russians who had overcome the Earth gravity and broken all the records:Yury Gagarin, the first astronaut; and Valery Brumel, the famous high jumper whose world record, 2m28cm, had not been beaten for more than 10 years.

...IN AUSTRALIA.

There were two wonderful draws, one after another, in Australian Oz Lotto 6+ 2 bonuses/45, on 27 April and 4 May, in which you could win a lot if you had a list of past drawings and carefully scrolled it looking for some repeating trends. And they did appear!

01-13-2004	02-05-25-29-36-42 +08-11	
01-20-2004	03-**12**-13-**23**-29-30 +18-37	< pay attention to 12, 23
01-27-2004	07-16-**21**-25-**26**-**38** +24-43	< pay attention to 21, 26, 38
02-03-2004	***07-12*-22-*26-32*-37 +24-*33***	< pay attention to 07, 12, 26, 32, 33
02-10-2004	10-19-29-37-41-43 +11-26	
02-17-2004	04-34-36-37-40-44 +01-35	
02-24-2004	10-11-23-24-26-39 +13-28	
03-02-2004	01-03-09-22-31-42 +04-10	
03-09-2004	08-**11**-14-23-29-44 +02-42	
03-16-2004	10-17-18-27-28-40 +05-29	
03-23-2004	04-08-12-13-29-44 +19-23	
03-30-2004	04-13-21-33-42-43 +14-19	
04-06-2004	**11**-15-19-23-37-41 +01-08	
04-13-2004	11-14-_15_-18-27-30 +06-39	
04-20-2004	05-**12**-_14_-**23**-36-39 +16-22	< **12 and 23** appeared again (2 WNs!)
04-27-2004	04-_13_-**21**-**22**-**38**-45 +11-**26**	< **21, 38, 26** appeared again after them (3 WNs!!)

05-04-2004   *07-11-12*-20-25-*32* +*26-33*   < **07, 12, 32, 26,
33** appeared after
them (5 WNs!!!)

AMAZING LINKED DISTANT REPEATING
CORRELATION illustrating in detail BRONZE RULE
#2, isn't it!

The L3H (Law of 3rd Hit) **dictated to** a player try all the
numbers from 02-03-2004 Draw in 05-04-2004 Draw due
to their incrising appearance from a previous draw to a new
one. Besides, a player could try 11 as a periodic X - - - X - - -
X number, number 20 according to SILVER RULE #1 after
21-22 in 04-27-2004 Draw and number 12 according to
GOLDEN RULE #3, number 32 according to SILVER
RULE #2, with 03 (23>13>03) and 14 (11>12>13>14) as the
equal candidates, with the only unpredictable but structural
(see again 20-21 in 04-27-2004 Draw) number 25.

That was a fantastic gift and lotto puzzle for all the Australian
lotto players. I wonder if someone saddled and tamed that
crazy lotto mustang..

…IN EUROPE.

EuroMillions is a less predictable lottery in my list of lotteries,
especially its 50 numbers on Blue balls. The numbers on the
Yellow balls are much more predictable with my MOG.
Below I have marked the results of 30 draws according to
the rules of the MOG.

16-29-32-36-41 +07-09	05-*06*-*16*-23-27 +06-07	24-26-31-38-50 +05-08
07-13-39-*47*-50 +02-05	15-*16*-21-*36*-38 +01-05	*07*-10-*27*-31-34 +03-08
14-18-19-31-*37* +04-05	01-03-21-32-39 +02-06	09-10-19-*37*-50 +01-06
04-*07*-33-*37*-39 +01-05	15-29-37-39-49 +04-09	05-15-24-35-44 +05-06
15-24-28-44-*47* +04-05	06-11-35-41-44 +05-06	20-27-41-43-50 +05-08
33-36-*37*-42-45 +04-09	09-13-34-41-42 +03-07	06-09-*10*-27-35 +06-08
03-04-10-23-43 +*02*-04	02-07-08-10-47 +01-07	01-*11*-22-28-44 +01-09
04-12-24-27-36 +*02*-09	02-23-28-40-43 +02-06	08-*12*-14-15-34 +06-07
01-04-10-19-23 +*02*-08	03-21-30-34-35 +01-02	
14-*15*-28-*35*-40 +01-03	04-23-*24*-28-*34* +01-03	
06-10-21-*45*-49 +03-05	02-0*5*-12-19-*44* +08-09	

A pathetic selection, isn't it? Almost nothing to make use of! No more than two WNs per a draw turning into just three when you take into account the structure of a previous draw.

...IN the UNITED KINGDOM.

The day I opened the site with the results of the UK national lottery Pick 6+bonus in 49 I was unpleasantly surprised to discover that there are several lotto machines with their own exotic names and sets of balls and that both of them are changed at random.

However, I decided to look closer through the past games not dividing the results into groups as if they were drawn by the only one lottery machine. **And imagine my next surprise** when I found that some draws could be predicted with my MOG!

Marked out as I usually do it with the Word menu options, the results look more predictable than in the case with Euro Millions.

867	01-03-22-32-38-44 +45	877	10-22-28-33-37-39 +42	890	06-08-21-25-43-47 +16
868	03-21-31-42-47-48 +34	878	01-04-05-25-34-46 +12	891	05-10-11-16-17-33+13
869	07-19-20-29-41-49 +18	879	11-15-18-24-34-44 +28	892	06-09-31-32-40-47 +24
870	01-03-04-05-17-37+30	880	01-04-06-18-19-40 +30	893	06-27-33-38-45-47 +08
871	01-03-26-34-43-47 +12	881	05-22-26-40-42-43 +44		
872	05-06-10-15-27-49 +20	882	05-08-09-26-29-44 +16		
873	23-32-33-42-43-45 +04	883	01-12-23-26-■-45 +43		
874	14-17-23-28-42-49 +05	884	07-22-■-44-48-49 +16		
875	10-11-15-18-19-40 +28	885	22-26-29-31-■-42 +06	*<4 WNs + bonus WN !!!*	
876	04-29-35-44-46-49 +12				

In Draw 885 some of players could even predict 29 if they picked it from the structural 20s (24, 28 in Draw 879 and 26, 29 in Draw 882), with 28 and 29 almost close to X - - X - - X pattern.

...IN the UNITED STATES.

It seems that there is nothing to explore and discover in the world of lotteries in the USA after Gail Howard with all her brilliant history, her books on the theme, her articles in newspapers, her infomercials on TV and her wondeful site with all the lottery stuff.

However, I found neither Pick 6 AWM-22/77 from the old Russian booklet nor something like my class of AWMs in the list of her Wheeling Systems in the Table of Contents of her book "LOTTO. HOW TO WHEEL A FORTUNE." Instead that in 2005, for the first time in my lotto practice, I came across US KENO with its 80 balls. Exploring its results I saw it was what I had always wanted. But living in Russia I couldn't reach it there. And I found such a KENO in Ukraine.

…IN UKRAINE.

Before 12 June 1991 Ukraine was one of the fifteen Soviet Republics. After that date it became an independent state with… online KENO, by the way, and it gave me a remarkable opportunity to plunge into it. My biggest wins were:8 in 10 once, 7 in 10 a few times and a lot of smaller prizes.

But the most terrific thing was when their KENO had a unique gathering of five XXX WNs in Draw 3607 (GOLDEN RULE #1). I was not ready to such a great event and, to my deepest regret, could win only one combination of the five golden numbers 07,14,26,30,37 in that draw.

Look at what rare gathering of 10 WNs happened then with 9 periodicals among them.

3593	03-08-12-16-**17-18**-....................................
3594	
3595	
3596	
3597	
3598	
3599	
3600	01-02-11-**17-18**-20-....................................
3601	
3602	
3603	01-10-11-18-20-21-24-27-35-**37**-**42**-43-46-61-64-66-**69**-74-76-78
3604	01-03-08-09-24-25-29-31-33-35-44-45-**48**-50-51-57-**69**-73-75-79
3605	02-04-**07**-**14**-22-23-**26**-**30**-**37**-39-**42**-43-**47**-48-61-62-63-66-**69**-80
3606	**07**-08-10-**14**-15-**26**-28-**30**-35-**37**-40-**46**-49-55-61-65-67-70-73-76
3607	05-**07**-13-**14**-**17-18**-24-**26**-29-**30**-**37**-39-**42**-**45**-47-52-57-**69**-74-75

...AND IN RUSSIA BUT TODAY.

For about 10 years already we have had renewed online lotteries on the site http://www.stoloto.ru/ with its English version https://en.stoloto.ru/

Among them there is Pick 5 from 36, Pick 6 from 45, Pick 6 from 49 + a bonus ball, Pick 7 from 49, TOP-3,

1-to-10-in-20-from-80 KENO, RAPIDO, JOKER and some others. As they were being introduced, I explored their results applying MOG rules to them and each time descovered that they were less or more predictable. I'll guide you through them after explaining you how to use PROG in selecting numbers for a new draw.

VITALLY NECESSARY PROG

Since the autumn of 2007 I have been armed with this special computer programme. I made up its algorithm and sent it to Mike, one of my most talented classmates, who, after graduating from the Novosibirsk State University in 1979, has been working as a programmer at the Novosibirsk Research Institute of Nuclear Physics. **And Mike in CVI invironment wrote the prog that in a few clicks can show a player the distribution of all MOG periodicals and other probable WNs within any group of draws in any desired color you can alter to your taste yourself.**

This is its main menu with the options I entitled myself and with Mike's copyright above. It's the third version of the programme.

◉ Lottery coincidence search © by MNK Oct 2009

File   D/T_hits   F+/-1   F_LDN   F+/-10   F_O/E
FS   Help!

Letter **F** in the titles of the options is the first letter of the verb **find.**

To make it work for yourself you need a database of between 2..100 draws of any lottery (except TOP-3). It must be copied into a simple notepad with as many draws as you select like in this one line example for our Joker lottery:8653,03 10 11 12 14 18 19 21 22 23 26 30 38 49 50

In which 8653 is the ordinal number of the draw and the rest 15 numbers are its WNs, with the obligatory comma after the draw number and two blank gaps between each two WNs.

Then, as usual, clicking on its executive file in the prog folder and selecting and after that clicking the necessary database from the list of them in the box that appears, you have the results of the draws in a new window under the menu waiting for your searching or selecting probable WNs for a new draw.

And now there is no comma after Darw 8653 but 4 blank gaps.

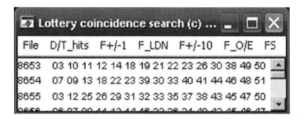

Clicking on **File** option, you see these suboptions:

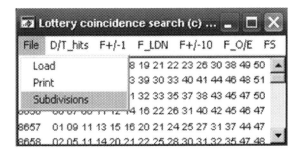

Clicking on **Subdivisions** you widen the draws to the full scale of 52 participating numbers:

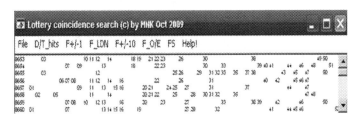

And a tick appears to the left of Subdivisions indicating your choice:√ **Subdivisions**.

Now you can see the structural differences among the draws inside 01..09/.../50..52 groups and the correlation in WNs among any of six groups within any two draws.

Clicking on **D/T_hits** you can see the ticks by default to the left of **Find Equality** and **Compare two strings** suboptions:

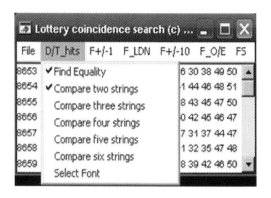

Now on the full-scaled playing field you can click on any two lines according to MOG periodical pattens XXX / X – X – X … so as you could see what repeating coinciding WNs will probably pop up in a new draw. Supposing wondering what numbers will come out in Draw 8658 I click on Draws 8656 and 8657 and I see the following marked picture:

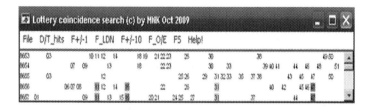

Awesome! I have 4 XXX candidates (11, 16, 31, 47) for Draw 8658. Are all of them hit? I don't know. **In the hierachy of MOG Rules, the Golden are the first ones to rely on,** even though you can think that 31 and 47 have already ended their hitting. From my rich lotto experience I can only assume that either no one or all four, with a few variants in between will probably hit. However for wheeling in one of my Joker AWMs they are at the top.

Then I click on Draws 8654 and 8656 to get X – X – X candidates.

And I have another 4 numbers:07, 22, 40, 46.

The database lacks Draw 8652 and it means I can't click on it and Draw 8655 to check X - - X - -X numbers. Never mind. We have our next **F+/-1** option with its **F+1** and **F-1** suboptions.

They help you to select GOLDEN RULE #3 numbers.

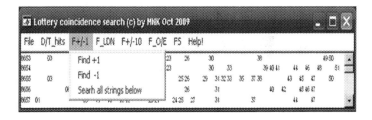

First click on **Find+1**. A tick will appear to the left of it. And a tick will also remain to the left of **Compare two strings** suboption under **D/T_hits**. Now click on Draw 8656 and you'll see this:

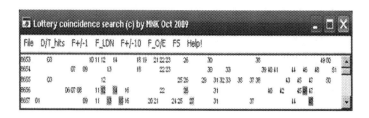

Now click on **Find-1**, then on Draw 8656 again and you'll have:

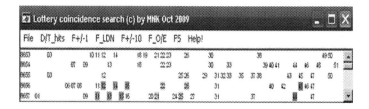

Now let's analyze and select the most probable descending numbers for our Draw 8658.

10 or **14**, or both of them have **double left-right weight**. So, they are strong candidates.

The double weight has also **12** and **16**, but it seems that **12** has already hit according to X-XX pattern in Draws 8653, 8655 and 8656.

From **20**, **24** and **28** candidates, **28** is special being part of **4 step slope** (25>26>27>28) and in Joker such **long left-right slopes** are often observed. Just look at 14>13>12>11 in Draws 8653-8656.

As for **43** and **48** candidates, **48** is like **28** being at the end of even longer slope. Such slopes are impressing and **28** and **48** are very impressive candidates.

Now let's look for Broken Periodicals (**BPs**) I showed you in GOLDEN RULE #2 and estimate their hitting. Among them the most frequent **BPs** are either **X-XX** or **XX-X**.

In that case our next candidates are **25**, **37** and **45**. Let's ignore **12** and **26** because they have already hit in Draws 8653, 8655 and 8656.

Now it's time to click on **F_LDN**, that is, Last Digit Number.

This option is for searching supplement numbers in the latest draw.

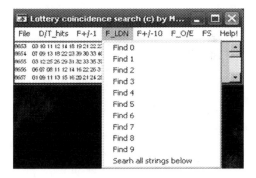

One by one, we should click on **Find 1**, **Find 5** and **Find 7** and then three times on Draw 8657.

This is the picture that PROG demonstrates you with LDN 5.

File	D/T_hits	F+/-1	F_LDN	F+/-10	F_O/E	FS	Help!

Then, according to SILVER RULE #3 our candidates for the next draw are **05**, **35**, **45**.

The other candidates are **41**, **07**, **17**.

Option **F+/- 10** helps us not to miss SILVER RULE #2 numbers. Click **F+10** and you'll see:

And our new candidates are **26** (06>16>26) and **31-34** (11-14 > 21-24 >31-34).

When you choose **Find -10** suboption, they are **06**, **11** and **27**.

The **F_O/E** (**Find odd/even** numbers) option is used more or less actively by me depending on the amount of more important GOLDEN or SILVER numbers selected for a new draw.

It's for finding BRONZE RULE #1 candidates.

Choose **Find odd** suboption and PROG shows the marked SNs in <u>01..09</u>/<u>10..19</u>/<u>20..29</u>/<u>30..39</u> groups. Too many groups, by the way!

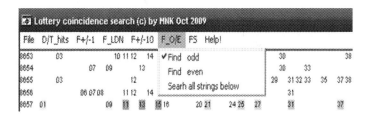

So, our odd/even candidates for Draw 8658 are:03-05-07/17-19/23-29/33-35-39

Comparing to **Find even** it is almost next to nothing:22-26-28

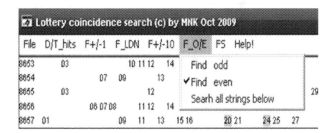

Adding them to each other, we have 13 SNs to be wheeled, to be on the safe side, in my 9/13/52 Joker AWM with 3 lines=3bets.

Well, so PROG has just helped us to choose all the candidates for a new draw but the question is which of them are more probable to appear in Draw 8658.

- ■ Let's estimate them group by group from the point of view of the **structural correlation between the latest (8657) and a new draw (8658).** By the structural correlation I mean the same amount of members or, may be, one or maximum two members more, in all the subdivisions of a lottery scope.

=> In that case in group <u>01..09</u> I would leave only 05 and 07 candidates because PROG chose them twice. They are the SNs that have **double weight**.

=> In group <u>10..19</u> I would bet on 10, 11, 14 and 16. Among them **10** and **14** are with **double weight** again:08>09>**10**<11<12 and 12>13>**14**<15<16. And 11 and 16 are XXX GOLDEN NUMBERS!

=> In group <u>20..29</u> I would bet on 20, 22, 24, 25 and 28.

=> In group <u>30..39</u> I would bet on 31, 35, 37 where **35** has **double weight.**

=> In group <u>40..49</u> I would bet on 46, 47, 48

- ■ Now we have the following line of 17 SNs to be wheeled in my Joker AWM for 17 SNs:

05-07-10-11-14-16-20-22-24-25-28-31-35-37-46-47-48

As you remember it has 6 horizontal lines and after wheeling gives us these bets:

1. 05-07-10-11-24-37-46-47-48
2. 05-07-10-11-14-25-28-31-35
3. 14-16-20-22-35-37-46-47-48
4. 05-07-10-11-14-16-20-22-24
5. 24-25-28-31-35-37-46-47-48
6. 05-16-20-22-24-25-28-31-48

■ I usually try to narrow my SNs betting on the most probable and +/-1 numbers around them.

It means that 46-**47**-48 are already MOG SNs but I must try with 30-**31**-32 too, waiting for 31 and 47 fourth hitting, which will probably be around them as I noticed with a lot of numbers repeatedly. Adding 11, 16 and 28 to them I can make up a bet set **11-16-28-30-31-32-46-47-48** and, as I often but not always do, check the bet set threefold.

■ JOKER is still the cheapest lottery in the list of RF (Russian Federation) online lotteries.

A bet in it costs 30 rur and this is its table of prizes:

WNs	PRIZES
4 in 9	a bet
5 in 9	2 bets
6 in 9	10 bets
7 in 9	1500 rur
8 in 9	9000 rur

9 in 9   Accumulating rising Jack Pot starting
with 200000 rur

■ Now we can look at the WNs that hit in Draw 8658
a year ago in October 2018, from where I copied
the database.

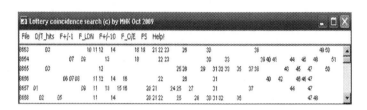

■ This is what we have after the calculating our wins:

=>In the bet **11**-16-**28**-**30**-**31**-**32**-46-**47**-**48** there are 7 WNs
x 3 = 4500 rur

=>In our 17 SNs **05**-07-10-**11**-**14**-16-**20**-**22**-24-**25**-**28**-**31**-
35-37-46-**47**-**48** there are 11 WNs.

1. **05**-07-10-**11**-24-37-46-**47**-**48** = 30 rur
2. **05**-07-10-**11**-**14**-**25**-**28**-**31**-**35** = 1500 rur
3. **14**-16-**20**-**22**-**35**-37-46-**47**-**48** = 300 rur
4. **05**-07-10-**11**-**14**-16-**20**-**22**-24 = 60 rur
5. **24**-**25**-**28**-**31**-**35**-37-46-**47**-**48** = 1500 rur
6. **05**-16-**20**-**22**-24-**25**-**28**-**31**-**48** = 1500 rur

■ **This was a detailed demonstration of what you
can get using all my lottery background and
tools in a draw.**

LOTTO RESEARCHING
WITH FS OPTION

The last option on the menu is **FS**. It enables a player to explore all the draws in a selected and downloaded database in order to find similar draws or **investigate the hitting of nonperiodic couples** in 01..09/10..19/ and the rest of the groups of a certain lottery.

Clicking on **FS** in the first two PROG versions you could see a new box appear near the results of the draws you had download into. It had 10 small vertical boxes with **N search** under them, a smaller box for selecting the amount of the numbers under your searching control and a couple of buttons **Go** and **Zero** which initiated and eliminated the content of the 10 boxes.

In the picture below you can see that I dragged and dropped the big box in the middle of the playing field of a group of Keno draws with its contracted to thirty one WNs to make it look more compact. Looking at the draws you can notice that numbers 24, 25, 28 tend to pop out together but how often? The option **FS** is the answer to this question. Placing them in the boxes (in any positions from the top to the bottom) and clicking **Go** we can see, as in the picture, how many times they have hit. Mind that on my screen the trio is inside yellow squares, as well as 03-04 and 07-08.

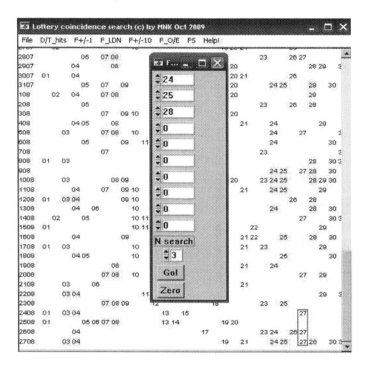

Why do we need to know that?

To bet on them in every next draw after their twice hitting, starting with Draw 908 (August 09) and expecting their new appearance. And here they are in Draws 1008, 1308 and 2708!

You can apply this method of searching to the other nonperiodic WNs, like with couples 03-04 and 07-08, where 07-08 demostrates even Golden Rule # 1 periodicity in Draws 2807, 108 and 508.

In selecting more similar WNs per a draw you can even go further! I said to myself once, "I wonder if at least two groups of nonperiodicals will encounter in a certain draw?" And look, they did:Couple **03-04** and Trio **24-25-28,** in Draw 2708.

That was another remarkable additional finding that PROG gave me!

Besides, the option **FS** gives you another researching opportunity. Setting 10 in **N search** box you can investigate the structural distribution of any 10 SNs on the area of the outcomes. But what was good for a maximum 10-number Keno bet set was not enough for wheeling more than 10 numbers in a wider AWM in a lottery. So, last autumn, in 2018, I asked Mihail to add 10 more boxes to have 20 of them, which suits most of AWMs because, as a rule, you don't need to wheel more than 20 SNs.

And now this modernized option allows you to manipulate with your SNs choosing and checking your various winning strategies.

And finally, **Help!,** which is not available in PROG yet.

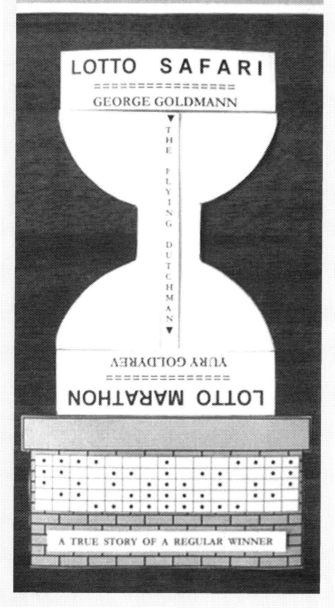

PART 2

LOTTO SAFARI

GEORGE GOLDMANN

▼
T
H
E

F
L
Y
I
N
G

D
U
T
C
H
M
A
N
▼

YURY GOLDYREV

LOTTO MARATHON

A TRUE STORY OF A REGULAR WINNER

To tell the truth, I had no real bets at that October Joker draw because at that time in Joker there was only a 15-minute interval between two draws but, mainly, because from September to May I teach my old and new students English. I work like a horse 7 days a week/up to 10 classes a day non-stop. So, I quite often have no time and, which is more important, extra energy for lotteries. It doesn't mean that I stop playing at all. I've always tried, especially on our school autumn, spring but, mostly, winter holidays between 30 December and 12 January. And do you remember what I am after in lotto hunting? Yes. It is SUPERGATHERING, which is the BEAUTY of CHANCE and this beauty is in the eye of the beholder.

INSTRUCTIVE PICK 6
FROM 45 TROPHIES

Before Keno was introdeced into RF online lotteries I played
Pick 5 in 36 and Pick 6 in 45 or 49+bonus and later Pick 7
in 49, also practicing Ukranian Keno online.

Since 2007 Mike's prog had always been at hand and using
it I generated my bet sets. In June 2010 I could have had
5 in 6 in the 6x45 lottery **by anology**. By anology, because
earlier, on April 21st, I hit 4 in 6 WNs (my win was **1064**
rur) making just two bets.

In this payslip I underlined them:**04, 11 17, 23.** Look how
easily I caught the WNs then.

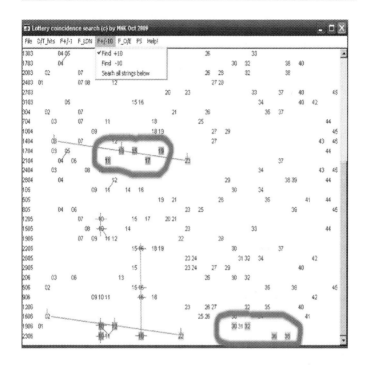

- As you can see in my first bet set (according to MOG) my SNs were:

03 as XXX pattern, 14 as 12>13>14 descending,

17 as the supplement odd member to 13, 15, x, 19 in Draw 1704

33, 43/ 35 as the supplement members to 03, 13 / 05, 15 with43 also as 45>44>43 candidate.

- In my second bet set my SNs were combined optimally:

04, on one hand, as a long distant correlative number after number 05 in Draw 1303, and on the other hand, as a gap number between 03 .. 05 WNs in the same draw,

11 and **17** as supplementing odd members of x-13-15-x-19 progression,

23 as **Find +10** selected number having **double weight 23** (03, 13 > **23**, 33,43), 39 as a long waited missing number and 43 as a double weight number.

But then, to my horror, at the end of June I discovered that I overlooked even better June 23 Draw analogical to April 21 Draw but with much higher winning chances.

Make sure of yourself and let's mourn it over with me!

- In it **10** was a WN after 10 in Draw 1906 according to the pattern in 1205 and 1505 Draws.

11 was a gap number after 10..12 in the previous draw.

22 as **Find +10** selected number like number **23** in 2104 Draw.

34, 36 and **38** were supplementing even members of 30-32-x-x-x progression. It is highly likely that I didn't try it in 2306 Draw because he had already hit earlier in 1606 Draw.

Powerful resemblance, isn't it, taking into account that, like with XXX number 03 in Draw 2104, XXX number 30 in Draw 2306 didn't hit, breaking The Law of the Third Hit.

Once, in November 2011, I was very close to the jackpot in Pick 6 from 45 lottery. Look what a beautiful parade of three MOG WNs that was, in the lottery which is less predictable than Keno, Rapido or Joker! And share my inner drama and tragedy of the situation in which I could afford only 100 rur for that draw at that time and, God is a witness, I almost did my best with my two bets again.

In the table below I have missed some draws and cut down all the numbers to 37 to narrow the playing scale.

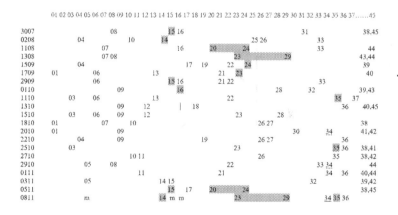

My two bets were 05-15-16-**34-35**-37 and 15-16-**23-34-35-36** (where **m** is missed).

WNs — Выпавшие номера: 36 14 35 29 23 34

Ваши номера: 34 23 15 16 35 36
My 2 bets — 05 15 16 37 34 35

	Совпавших комбинаций	Выигрыш		
Совпало	комбинаций	Трид, руб.	Сумма, руб.	
3	1	2 652	2 652	
5	1	50	50	

I put 37 in the 05-15-16-**34-35**-37 bet according to the probable descending 35 > 36 > 37 expectation. But the second bet set was almost perfect. It could be more perfect if I tried **14** instead of 15, as the number that hit after 15 in Draw 0208; or **29** instead of 16, as a linked what-after-what number in 23 -29 couple which hit in Draws 1308 and after the same 20-24 couple in Draw 0208.

In the end, the periodicals **34-35-36** (Golden Rile # 1) demonstrated the triumph of my MOG in its LAW of THE THIRD HIT! **Incredible, it's hard to believe but such a rare event occurred.**

To comment a bit further, 35 had X - - - - X - - - -X pattern. Such a pattern and even twice higher you can encounter in Pick 5 and Pick 6 lotteries, so it's important not to ignore them weighing the probability of your SNs.

SHORT-TERM DIVING IN RAPIDO

Doing justice it should be said, though, that at their beginning and for about two years all our online lotteries were almost equally available to all categories of players. So, when RAPIDO was introduced, I tried it and had wins, too. I liked it and still enjoy its 8 in 20 formula with such a table of prizes at that period when a bet set price was 60rur:

WNs	PRIZES
4+1 in 8	a bet=60rur
5 in 8	2 bets
5+1 in 8	5 bets
6 in 8	600rur
6+1 in 8	1800rur
7in 8	3000rur
7+1 in 8	9000rur
8 in 8	60000rur
8+1	60000rur +accumulating rising Jack Pot

Plus one bonus number is 1,2,3 or 4 number from an additional area on a bet card.

And MOG proved that RAPIDO was more predictable than KENO. Take a look at what beautiful SUPERGATHERING of 7WNs occurred in the lottery in Draw 2104 on Febuary 26, 2017.

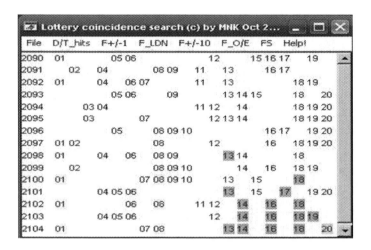

Six periodicals—01,08,13,14,16,18—and 20 as a four stepped right descending number! Some of them had double weight, by the way, and a triplet—14,16,18—demonstrated XXX golden pattern! And just look at the playing field above, at Draw 2095, at another left descending number 03 and periodic numbers 13,14,18,19,20. And above all, what a marvellous concentration of the same numbers in a group of draws when you have an opportunity to select 8 from 20!!!

And where was I with my MOG in that February? At the lessons, of course, curse them all!

However, despite my regular 9-month tiresome but rewarding tutoring, on January 05 and 17, 2018 I managed to hit 6 in8=600rur and 6+1 in8=1800rur in this lottery making only one bet again, as it is in 80% cases with me. This is how it was.

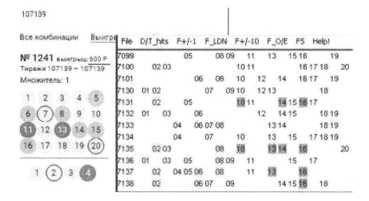

In the picture you can see the marked distribution of WNs before Draw 107139 (mind that I deleted 10 in each ordinal number of the draws). I wish I could focus on 07, as 05>06>07 number, instead of 11 or 13, which didn't hit.

My win on January 17 was luckier but, as I can see it now, could have had 7+1 in8 result.

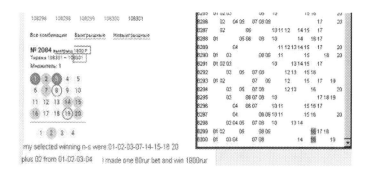

Obviously, I should have tried 08 instead of 01 in one more bet set inside the patterned 07-08 couple, because it had hit in the group of 03-07-08 WNs in the draws above!

Now that a bet set costs 150rur and the prizes are 3 times higher, I am licking my juicy mouth looking forward to new terrific outcomes of this type of a lottery. I hope I'll come back to it some day.

PRAISEWORTHY KENO PEARLS

Nevertheless, only when summer comes, I am eager and psychologically ready to set out for my much more numerous lotto trophies.

KENO was put on the site only in the middle of March, 2011. Its 80 numbers were drawn by a random numbers generator, and at the very beginning I thought that it was useless to try it. To my great surprise, however, after searching the results of a few first draws I discovered that MOG could be applied to selecting WNs for it, too, as though all the 80 numbers were drawn by a real lottery machine. That was so promising and exciting that I started my prolonged RF Keno hunt. To my regret, I could not play in each draw again. So, naturally, I simply overlooked the draws where MOG could bring me bigger wins.

And for 6 summers Keno was my favorite, as it was the most predictable and the cheapest lottery in which a bet cost 10 rur for a long time. The situation changed in the spring of 2018 when it began to cost 50 rur. In Keno they also changed the interval between two draws dramatically, starting with 2 draws a day and ending in a 15-minute interval. For the 7 years PROG gave me an excellent opportunity of starting and constantly enlarging my collection of best Keno draws in which unique or super gathering of WNs were filed by me in 3 folders:One-Group Gathering, Gathering of Periodicals, Stepped Slopes and Periodicals Gathering. Look at them closer in the illustrations.

One-Group Gathering (5 WNs inside 10..19 group) on June 30, 2015

Lottery coincidence search (c) by MHK Oct 2009							
File	D/T_hits	F+/-1	F_LDN	F+/-10	F_O/E	FS	Help!
47135	02 03 04	06 07			15		20 21 22
47136	01		12	15	18 19		23
47137	04	06 07	12 13	15	17		22 23
47138		06	10 11	15 16			
47139	02		10	15	17	21	
47140	04		10 11 13 14		18		
47141	02		09 10 11 12	15	18	21	
47142	03		09 10 11	16	18	21	

Gathering of Periodicals on August 14, 2017

File	D/T_hits	F+/-1	F_LDN	F+/-10	F_O/E	FS	Help!
6924	01 02	05 06		12	15		
6925	03		08	12	14 15	17	
6926	04 05		09	11	13	17	
6927				13 14	16		
6928	02	05			15 16	18	
6929			10	12	16		
6930	02	05 06	11	14			
6931	01	05 06	12	13			
6932	04 05	09			18		
6933				13 14	15 16	18	
6934	02	04	08 09 10		15	18	
6935		08		14			
6936	04 05 06 07 08	10 11	13	15	18		

Stepped Slopes and Periodicals
Gathering on August 24, 2015

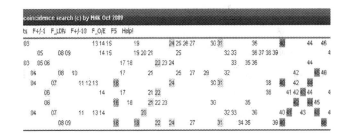

You absolutely need to have such a collection to brush up your selecting lotto skills and get used to most unbelievable anomalies in WNs hitting.

To begin with, when Keno balls were drawn 2 times a day, at 9am and 9pm, I had that beautiful 5 in 5 win repeated twice on June 12, 2014 at 9p.m local time, within a group of eight doubled bets.

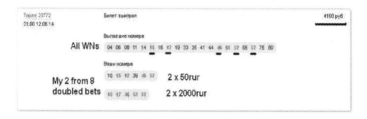

It's a pity I didn't use AWMs in that draw of quite a rare gathering as you can see below:

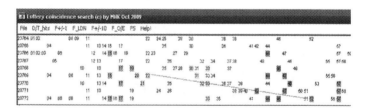

WNs **15** and **17** had **double weight** (after 11, 13, x, x, 19 in 23771 Draw and being Golden WNs).

46 was at the end of the right-pointed arrow-head pattern: "**>**"

52 was at the end of 22>32>42>**52** ten+ succession. **57** hit as a classic XXX number.

If I were not a poet of HIS MAJESTY the CHANCE, I would be much cooler and more rational and bet on these 5 WNs tenfold or, at least, fivefold.

But I am what I am and I am slowly moving to my biggest wins. Moreover, it seems to me for a long time that CHANCE the GIANT, an old man with million faces and actually my Saint Patron, has always blinded me a little at a lot of the moments of my reaching the top lottery prizes, allowing me to get the third and the second ones exclusively, as if constantly checking my loyalty to him and waiting for the end of my another half fictional half true Russian-English manuscript about two of us and HIS PROFOUND INFLUENCE on our lives.

И, кажется, рассвет вставал	It seemed it was the
Или закат сходил,	crack of dawn
А я всё шёл, я всё шагал	Or sunset with last flash.
Всё выше восходил.	And I stepped up and up and up
	And higher, to ascend
Туда, где среди трёх вершин	
Я купол разглядел	Where amidst the lonely peaks
И там, в кругу колонн, один,	I spotted a huge dome.
Как истукан, сидел...	And there, inside the colonnade,
Сидел огромнейший старик.	In kind of a pharaoh's throne,
Без чёткого лица,	Without a clear distinct face,
Морщинки, складки,	An old giant slightly drowsed,
властный лик -	His wrinkles, eyelids,
Менялись без конца.	bushy brows
	In their kaleidoscopic phase,
И перед ним очаг мерцал,	
Предвестник темноты	The warming hearth
И он в раздумье созерцал	in front of him,
Объёмный огненный	The friendly source of light,
кристалл	And he, in meditation, swung
И отблеск пламени смещал	At times from side to side.
Ещё сильней черты.	And flicking flame much
	more displaced
	His facial features flight.

И, обернувшись на шаги,	At hearing my steps behind,
Он свой процесс прервал.	His contemplation died.
Широким жестом всей руки	By a cordial gesture of his arm
На место указал,	My seat, he specified,
И голосом глухой тайги	And in the voice of wild taiga
Под сводом зазвучал.	At a thunderbolt, he cried:
"А-аа,	"HA!
ВОТ И ТЫ,	HERE YOU ARE,
ПОКЛОННИК МОЙ,	ADEPT of MINE,
БРОДЯЧИЙ ДИЛЕТАНТ,	MY WANDERING
МОЙ ВИРТУОЗ	DILETTANTE,
ПОЛУЖИВОЙ,	MY VIRTUOSO,
ЗАКОПАННЫЙ ТАЛАНТ.	SCARCELY LIVE,
	SO LOTTERY TALENTED!
ПРИСЯДЬ С ДОРОГИ,	
ОТДОХНИ.	SIT DOWN AND
СЫГРАЕМ В ЧЁТ-НЕЧЁТ.	RELAX A BIT.
А-а...ТЯЖКО, ЧТО	IN TALKS IS HAPPINESS.
Ж НЕ ГОВОРИ	EXHAUSTED? DON'T
Я ЗНАЮ НАПЕРЁД	SPEAK, INDEED
НЕХИТРЫХ МЫСЛЕЙ	I KNOW THE PROCESS
ТВОИХ БЕГ	OF SIMPLE THOUGHTS
В ЗЕМНОМ МОЁМ РАЮ...»	of YOURS
	IN MY...MY EARTHLY
"Прости, отец,	PARADISE."
но что-то я тебя не узнаю...»	
	"But sorry, FATHER,
	who are you?
	I cannot recognize."

Back to Keno, while I was having English classes with my students during my autumn, winter and spring months, often leaving home at 11 am and coming back at 10pm, often in my thoughts, I kept on planning to get multiwins without spending my time thinking over each draw. In Keno, for instance, a bet set can be played from 1 to 5, 10, 20, 30, 50 and to 100 drawings.

In such an approach to lottery games there is an obvious advantage of saving your time and focusing it on something else rather than lotteries. There have always been some players who bet on their specific SNs and finally a year or years later they used to win a fortune. But the problem with me is that I have always been rather economical, even mean, spending no more than 300 rur per a draw, with the idea the fewer the safer. **Perhaps, it's because my best wins have never cost me a lot.**

In short, for the first time in my lotto practice, on September 25, 2016, late in the morning I picked these 16 Keno numbers:02-03-05-10-11-12-20-21-31-33-35-37-39-60-67-68, wheeled them in my smallest Keno 10/16/80 AWM and sent them for playing within 20 draws (from 85985 to 86004) spending 800 rur (10 rur x 4 x 20).

No sooner had I stepped outdoors than the prize avalanche broke out. During 5 hours, while I was giving my private lesson after lesson or walking from home to home, I was receiving my next lotto sms on my mobile phone adding the number of my wins and getting more and more excited. There were 19 of them in the end.

And late in the evening I told my wife that I was the winner of the day with 3000 rur income from my eight students and 6940 rur in Keno wins. Inside the wins the picture was the following:

Draw 85986=> 0 in10=20rur / **Draw 85989**=> 5 in10=20rur and **8 in10=5500**rur /

Draw 85991=> 5 in10=20rur and 6 in10 threefold=3x100rur / Draw 85994=> 0 in10=20rur /

Draw 85997=> 5 in10 twofold=2x20rur and 6 in10=100rur / Draw 85998=> 0 in10=20rur /

Draw 86000=> 0 in10=20rur / Draw 86001=> 5 in10 twofold=2x20rur

Draw 86003=> 5 in10=20rur, 6 in10 twofold=2x100rur and **7 in10=600**rur

From the list of 25 draws above the wins you can see that I started with Draw 85951 and played actively for another 4 draws ending in 85955 and then only 30 draws later I took part in those 20 games. It means that I selected my numbers so carefully that they, having been wheeled in the AWM optimally, brought me TWO MAXIMUM WINS WITHIN NOT TOO LARGE AMOUNT OF GAMES. In addition to them, earlier in Draw 85951 I had made two bets and won 5 in8=100rur. And in Draw 85954 my only bet brought me 0 in7=20 rur win.

85951	85952	85953	85954	85955	85985	85986	85987
85988	85989	85990	85991	85992	85993	85994	85995
85996	85997	85998	85999	86000	86001	86002	86003
86004							

Все ставки   Выигрышные   Невыигрышные

А	А
5	1
из	из
8	7

№ 280   № 269
100 Р.

To sum up, on that September 26 I had a daily earning of 10060rur.

Just for comparison, the sum is 500rur higher than my monthly pension as a retired teacher now and it is also equal to our family's monthly payment for our 3-room flat with two balconies.

And at last in 2017, in August, <u>there was a culmination of my KENO wins:I had almost 100 of them!!!</u>

On August 08 I gained this trophy, hitting 7 in 10 WNs (2x 600rur) twice:

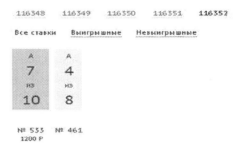

On August 17 there was the whole sparkling of them in Draw 117214.

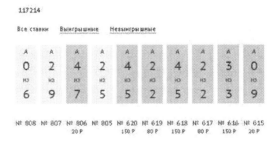

A week later, on August 26, there was the similar case, with these five out of eighteen total wins.

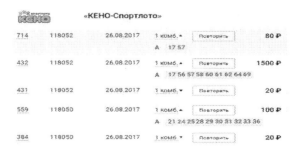

I can't remember now why I didn't wheel them then?

Just imagine:6 in 10 WNs in Bet Set 559 and 7 in 9 WNs in Bet Set 432. And all the WNs are from different playing groups inside the 80 playing numbers! What prevented me from putting them together:21-**24 25**-28-**29 30 31 32**-33-36 + **17**-56-**57 58 60 61 62**-64-**69** and wheel them, as they are, in my Keno AWM for 18 SNs, without number 21 as a lonely number having no "+/-1" neighbors.

24	25	28	29	30	31	32	33	36	17	56	57	58	60	61	62	64	69
•	•		•	•	•	•			•		•	•	•	•	•		•
▼	▼		▼	▼	▼	▼			▼		▼	▼	▼	▼	▼		▼
•	•	•	•	•									•	•	•	•	•
•	•	•			•	•					•	•			•	•	•
•	•				•	•	•	•	•	•	•					•	•
		•	•		•	•	•		•	•	•			•	•		
		•		•	•	•		•	•		•	•	•		•		
•			•	•			•	•	•	•			•	•			•

Bet Set 1:**24 25**-28-**29 30**-**60 61 62**-64-**69** = 8 in 10 win = 5500 rur

Bet Set 2:**24 25**-28-**31 32**-**57 58**-**62**-64-**69** = 8 in 10 win = 5500 rur

Bet Set 3:**24 25**-**32**-33-36-**17**-56-**57**-64-**69** = 6 in 10 win = 100 rur

Bet Set 4:28-**29**-**31 32**-33-56-**57 58**-**61 62** = 7 in 10 win = 600 rur

Bet Set 5:28-**30 31 32**-36-**17**-**57 58 60 62** = 8 in 10 win = 5500 rur

Bet Set 6:**24**-**29**-**30**-33-36-**17**-56-**60**-**61**-**69** = 7 in 10 win = 600 rur

No doubt, CHANCE the GIANT interfered secretly again in this bloodless endless competitive combat between two of us! But rather than probable I wouldn't have used my AWMs because of that too short 15- minute Time Interval I had for picking SNs for that draw. You see, the results appeared on the site 2 minutes later after their drawing. Then I had to copy them into the current Keno database, which occupied another 2 minutes. Then I had to open PROG and start clicking on its options. Then, deciding on employing an AWM, I had to spend some time on that and, above all, I had to be at the very irritating edge of overtiming.

Surely, despite this serious obstacle, with Keno I made enough hay while the sun shone.

Derek also didn't lose his chance with it. This is what he wrote to me in one of his emails:

"I'm still playing the daily Keno here in Ontario and occasionally in Quebec…won a few 7/10's and 8/10's but not the BIGGEE 10/10 yet…it's probably just around the corner. Who knows, Yury! We both know you can't win it if you're not in the game no matter what method you invent. Using Gail Howard's software and coming up with ways to use the numbers to my advantage that Gail never thought about. BTW>>>she died last October 2015 but her Office maintains the software and lottery updates, so all remains steady on the lottery front of updates."

That was a sad news about Gail, my lottery elder sister. And it was not steady on the RF lottery front, either. They changed it to the worst for us players increasing fivefold the cost of a Keno bet, lessening the proportion expense/win in all the categories in the table of their prizes, in fact, sawing off the bough they were sitting on, and, hence, scaring away many Keno devotees like me. I had to adapt to the situation again and I switched to JOKER and, more actively, to TOP-3.

BIRTHDAY DATES
PROBING IN JOKER

The date when JOKER drew my attention is inside its folder on my old PC. It was at the end of August, 2018. Actually they introduced it earlier but it was me who did not have time to pay attention to its resemblance to KENO. But when I discovered that I didn't need to deal with cards themselves but only with their ordinal numbers from 1 to 52, JOKER's hour struck. And here is part of a screenshot of my exactly first JOKER wins on August 23, 2018.

"Una herunda ver not facit!" quoted I this Latin proverb to myself (one swallow doesn't make spring) and, ispired, I continued.

However, making up a JOKER database was a boring time-consuming occupation. That is why, just for fun, I decided to check my lotto luck with our family nine birthday dates. I selected mine, my wife's, our both daughter's, their husbands' and their children's. In a rising progression they are the following:03-04-13-16-17-20-21-22-30.

Seeing the numbers grouping with four close member clusters 03-04, 16-17, 20-21 and 21-22 while scrolling the results of JOKER draws downloaded into PROG, I made up my mind that they had had high chances to hit. Choosing the interval of 20 draws again, like in my example with KENO multidraws, on Septermber 26 I did the first injection, so to say, into Draws 7013 to 7042. It cost me 600rur (30rurx20draws) and in the end my catch was 360rur.

"Not bad for the first time," thought I and on December 09, 2018 I did the second intervention. It was more rewarding, as 7 numbers hit and only 2 missed in Draw 12709. The missing numbers were my wife's birthday (04) and our elder daugher's husband's (21). Kidding over the result, I remember attacking my wife with the question, "Well, who is the weakest family link?"

The black and white picture doesn't show the true colors of the cards. Leave Card 4 and Card 21 in their whites and color the rest of the cards in a light tanned body and you'll have appoximately what I see on the screen. My total win was 660rur in those draws.

So, this passive lotto strategy is quite admissible and, as I commented it above, does bring prizes to those who can wait, having to bet or preferring betting on some unchangeable SNs.

FROM RADIANT WINS
TO TOP-3 WAGES

"Today, on August 18, 2013, when I am writing these lines, our TOP-3 lottery has its second online anniversary. It is drawn 2 times a day:at 1 p.m. and at 1 a.m. Today at 1 a.m. it is going to be its 1442 draw. The prizes are going to be much higher. The prize fund with about 2 000000 rur will be added and distributed among its winners. I am going to take part in it, of course. But let's see what prizes I can get, and if MOG also works with this sort of a lottery." wrote I six years ago planning to submit the manuscript of this book that year. **The worst thing was that the numbers were also drawn by a random number generator (RNG)!**

A bet set was 10 rur then and a player could hit one, two or three WNs on a playing patch consisting of 3 vertical rows of from 9 to 0 numbers in the direction from the top to the bottom. There were only 4 categories of prizes:50 rur for exactly one WN in any of the 3 rows, 500 rur for exactly two WNs in any two rows, 250 rur for two WNs in their direct or back order (3-5-x / 5-3-x) and 5000 rur for exactly there WNs.

It was the lottery where I didn't need to use PROG and it saved my time for picking my SNs. I liked it immediately and, despite my apprehension of randomly drawn numbers, a few first groups of draws with their WNs demostrated their hitting according to MOG rules and also this or that giving-a-high-hope case of gathering—and sometimes even supergathering—in a draw.

This is what the draws disclosed.

September 2012			December 2012				June 2013	
28	4-7-6	(-7-6)	02	3-2-6	(3-2-)		26	5-7-9
28	8-8-6	(-8-6)	02	4-2-5	(4-2-)		26	4-3-9
29	5-9-6	(-9-6)	03	5-2-8	(5-2-)		27	5-7-7
							27	6-4-9

Here, by the way, I made three bets on **2**, and two bets on **5-2**. **My win was 3x50+2x500 = 1150 rur**

June – July 2013		August 2013		September 2012		May 2011	
28	3-6-5	02	3-7-6	03	6-7-9	13	6-3-3
28	3-0-6	03	6-5-2	04	6-6-9	13	6-6-3
29	1-6-3	03	0-0-9	04	7-1-3	14	2-3-5
29	9-1-5	04	1-2-6	05	8-3-9	14	9-3-3
30	3-3-7	04	3-6-9				
30	5-0-1	05	2-9-1				
01	8-6-8	05	1-4-6				
01	9-5-2						
02	3-4-4						

Practically, the same MOG periodicals and descending +/-1 WNs, aren't they? I continued with my careful observation and soon it brought positive results. MOG worked with TOP-3, too!

The frequently observed WNs patterns were also like these:

August 2013		June 2013		July 2013	
22	9-6-**2** - - **2**	27	5-7-7	12	6-2-6
22	0-**2**-**2** - **2** -	27	**6**-4-9	13	**1**-6-0
23	**2**-2-**2** **2** - -	28	3-**6**-5	13	1-**1**-4
		28	3-0-**6**	14	6-5-**1**

I didn't hit exactly 3 WNs at that time but I had quite enough 500 rur wins to keep on playing.

It was my younger daughter Helen who nearly hit 3 WNs once in the brilliant November 13 Draw in 2012. This is, by the way, one of the brightest lotto examples in my TOP-3 collection of fantastic anomalous hitting and of what you can get employing MOG.

NOVEMBER 2012

01	4 8 8	05	2 6 6	10	6 1 5			
01	**0** 5 4	05	8 0 0	10	4 2 **3**			
02	3 0 9	06	**7** 4 4	11	1 9 6			
02	6 7 8	06	2 1 6	11	**0** 8 **3**	0		3
03	**0** 3 8	07	4 1 9	12	5 **0** 9		0	
03	8 1 9	07	**7** 6 2	12	**0** *1* **3**	0	1	3
04	8 5 9	08	4 8 0	13	**0** 2 **3**	0	2	3
04	**0** 0 1	08	9 5 5		**So, two MOG rules give us all the 3 WNs!**			
		09	**7** 8 8		**How do you like that?**			
		09	8 0 2					

You can see that from the very beginning of November there appeared MOG WNs, **0** and **7**, which you could easily bet on. Then, as a prelude to the fabulous November 13 Afternoon Draw, number **3**, obeying the LAW of the THIRD HIT, popped out in November 12 Evening Draw.

Just not to lose, I did 2 bets on it that evening and won 100 rur.

But the next day I went to work early and couldn't play in November 13 Afternoon Draw. At 1:30 p.m. Helen called me on my cellphone while I was walking down the street to my next student and enthusiastically but then with a deep sorrow in her voice informed me that she won 2000 rur.

She had doubled me logging into my lotto account and she made only 4 bets, with each bet bringing her 500 rur, placing two bets on **0** and **2** and another two bets on **2** and **3.**

Тираж 893
10:00 13.11.12

Билет выиграл

Выпавшие номера

WNs: 0 2 3

Ваши номера

Helen's SNs: 0 2 —

— 2 3

"Why didn't you bet on the three of them?" I shouted into the mobile," If only for one bet!" But I knew her answer. I myself was the reason of her choice having taught her before that better a small fish than an empty dish.

Another fantastic gathering of three WNs was on August 24 in the morning draw that I had to skip. On its eve my wife and I were invited by our younger daughter to her son's birthday. Besides, after the occasion we had to visit our elder daughter in a hospital, where she stayed with our second grandson who had been operated on. So, my wife and I were

very tired that night and I didn't download the results of
August 23rd afternoon (2-2-2) and early morning (2-1-6)
draws.

18 2-7-**5**
18 6-5-8
19 4-3-8
19 3-9-7
20 4-0-5
20 1-1-4
21 3-6-**5**
21 5-7-4
22 9-6-**2**
22 0-**2-2**
23 **2-2-2**
23 **2-1**-6
24 **2-0-5**

And look how CHANCE the GIANT
punished me.

*I laid half of my life on that and I wasn't
there at the right moment!*

*Only one and a half day break from lotteries
and such a bitter disappointment of what I
lost!*

Looking at the distribution of prizes in August
23rd afternoon draw I saw that 73 winners hit
2-2-2 WNs. It meant that lottery players hunted for such
outcomes as 0-0-0/1-1-1…9-9-9 and always made a lot of
bets on them.

On the other hand, there were only 3 winners with **2-0-5**
WNs in August 24th afternoon draw and that, in its turn,
meant that I AM AMONG JUST A FEW LOTTO GURU
WHO HAS THIS KIND of KNOW-HOW!!!

*As you can see, The Law of the Third Hit, discovered by me,
revealed itself in its best brilliance in these two unique
draws. But the creator of the MOG and the discoverer of
the Law himself turned out to be a bad executor, though
this time due to insurmountable obstacles on his lottery
path.*

The TURNING POINT in TOP-3
happened in the middle of July, 2018.

A bet set had been raised to 60 rur and the table of prizes became enlarged to 11—much more attractive—categories of prizes. Unfortunately, the interval between two draws was shortened to 15 minutes as in KENO

Cat-s	WNs in a bet set.	Prizes (rur)
1	Any 1 exactly	300
2	Any 2 (left-right/right-left)	1500
3	First 2 exactly	3000
4	Last 2 exactly	3000
5	Any 3	5000
6	Any 3 (any 2 are twins)	10000
7	Exactly 3+Any 3	17500/2500
8	Exactly 3+Any 3 (any 2 are twins)	20000/5000
9	Exactly 3	30000
10	Combo 1 (3 WNs bet sets)	30000
11	Combo 2 (6 WNs bet sets)	30000

And the turning point was in the fact that I introduced my new revolutionary TOP-3 searching tool. It sounds strange but before that date I didn't have the need to use it. **It was a spreading map (SM) with 0 to 9 horisontal positions for WNs**, which were represented with the same black spots as in my AWMs. And such a map became a powerful means of investigation of the concealed distribution of WNs.

Supposing that you have these August 30th results of a few night draws:

1) 677, 2) 634, 3) 821, 4) 716, 5) 877, 6) 669, 7) 587

Let's put them into this table, marking their hitting on the spreading map:

WNs		0	1	2	3	4	5	6	7	8	9
6 7 7	>							●	%		
6 3 4	>				●	●		●			
8 2 1	>		●	●						●	
7 1 6	>		●					●	●		
8 7 7	>								%	●	
6 6 9	>							%			●
5 8 7	>						●	m	●	●	

The sign "%" shows that a number hit twice in one of the 0 to 9 positions and "m" is missed.

The WNs in the last draw are absolutely predictable according to MOG:

5 to the left of 8 and 7 (as 7>6>**5** descending);

8 as X-X-X pattern (see its vertical position on the spreading field);

7 as double weight of XX-X and X - - X - - X patterns,

6 as a quite probable XX-X-XX number, which actually missed.

Keeping in mind Principle of Equality of outcomes, we must wheel all the 4 SNs in this matrix and choose *Category 5* at making our bets:

5	6	7	8	
●	●		●	
●		●	●	= 5000 rur
●	●	●		
	●	●	●	

Hence, spending 60x4=240 rur we have 5000rur win.

Having an opportunity to spend more per a draw and wishing to hit exactly 3 WNs to get 30000, you could assume that **5** will appear first (from left to right) among WNs. In such a case you could add to it either 07-08 or 08-07 and celebrate the win. The problem is that it could appear in the middle positon with the same 7>6>5 descending. So, the 5-6-7-8 wheeling was the cheapest control of the SNs coming to the optimum win.

Now that you are reading these lines, the whole exercise book has already been filled with the spreading maps on each page since that time. Let's look into this TOP-3 laboratory, at the most thrilling results of WNs gathering and what I managed to do with what CHANCE the GIANT tossed up for us, his lotto fans, and puzzled us with.

Before making bets I always copy the results of the last 10 to 15 draws. Late at night on July 26, 2018 they were the following:

LT	MNs	0	1	2	3	4	5	6	7	8	9
21:55	1 2 8		•	•						•	
22:10	3 9 6				•			•			•
22:25	0 1 2	•	•	•							
22:40	9 9 2				•						%
22:55	9 6 4					•		•			•
23:10	1 1 5		%				•				
23:25	0 2 5	•		•			•				
23:40	3 7 3				%				•		
23:55	5 6 2			•			•	•			
0:10	2 7 9			•					•		•
0:25	0 1 5	•	•				•				
0:40	5 7 9			m			•		•		•

I had 3 periodic candidates "2-5-7" for "0:40" Draw.

It looked as if 7 (X-X-X) went in the middle position (and it hit there, as you can see),

5 went in the right position, and 2 – in the left one by correlation with the WNs in the previous draw. That was my first bet set, by the way.

But my second bet set was based on the assumption that 5-7-9 would hit. Why? **Observing TOP-3 draws for a long time I noticed the close connection between any new draw and two last ones.** You can easily find it even in the July 26 list of draws. For example, WNs **1** and **2** in "22:25" Draw are from "21:55" Draw, as well as WNs **5** and **2** in "23:55" Draw are from "23:25" Draw. Therefore, for the "0:40" Draw I had the following candidates from the two previous draws:0-1-2-5-7-9. Divided into two halves, they could be low (0-1-2) and high (5-7-9) SNs. I simply decided to check the high SNs in my second bet set by *Category 5* and…they hit!

| 26.07.2018 | 1 комб. ▲ | Повторить | 5000 ₽ |
| | А 5 7 9 | | |

That was a promising start and after that, as my winning statistic shows on the site, I had the other 17 wins, including last two *Category 2* wins by August 26.

LT	WNs
14:40	**7 4** 8
15:40	0 2 **2**
15:55	**7 4 2**
16:10	**7 4 2**

But three day before that, on August 23, at 16:10, **I skipped this amaizing supergathering!**

It was just because I left my desk with the current results and went to the kitchen to have a bite feeling hungry. The 1st surprising thing with it was that it didn't need the SM. And the 2nd unexpected thing was that it occurred after an hour's schedule RNG break. But the 3rd unforgettable fact nearly killed me:it twinned the previous draw, though **7 4** had illustrated GOLDEN RULE #2 hitting. How many times would you bet on three of them, I wonder?

And on September 08, I could have had a wonderful win too. But this time it was Helen, my younger daughter again, who inadvertently deprived us of, at least, _Category 5 prize_ on that day.

I had some free time on that late Saturday afternoon and I disposed to play for about two hours. By "17:10" Draw I had put down the results of the last 13 draws on a new page and rolled out the playing field to the right of them, when suddenly—Helen arrived with Nastya, our youngest grandkid. They stayed with us for more than an hour and we had fun with them, but look what we all lost!

LT	MNs	0	1	2	3	4	5	6	7	8	9
16:25	6 6 0	●						%			
16:40	3 2 8			●	●					●	
16:55	1 9 7		●						●		●
17:10	4 6 2			●		●		●			
17:25	8 7 3				●				●	●	
17:40	4 0 2	●		●		●					
17:55	1 5 7		●	m		m	●	m	●		

The numbers 1, 5 and 7 were my astrological numbers:1-7 my b/d and -57 the year of it!

And what the Beauty of Chance occured! Two multistepped left-right slopes (1 and 5) and X-X-X periodical (7). The other periodical candidates 2-4-6 were not as exciting as 1-5-7, though being a serious alternative needed trying due to their marked strong positions on the list of draws.

"CHANCE the GIANT cast them at the time when I was not ready to get them. It's unfair." thought I that night shaking my head, "On the other hand, I would never make out the combination on the vertical list of the results without such a smart presentation of WNs!"

With the new 2019 year, however, there came a higher tide of my TOP-3 wins. On January 05, during winter holidays, I added the next *Category 2* exhibit to my TOP-s collection of prizes.

▶ It is very important to show a few examples of various patterns of BRONZE RULE #2, which, for this sort of a lottery, is a close resemblance of positional grouping between WNs separated by some draws. There can be observed quite a variety in the frame of the rule.

27. 05. 2019	01. 08. 2018	13. 08. 2018	27. 07. 2018	16. 08. 2018	**18.** **08.** **2018**	**01.** **06.** **2019**	**11.** **06.** **2019**
1 1 6	5 6 8	1 5 0	2 6 8	3 1 3	9 1 4	6 8 7	9 1 8
8 2 7	1 5 4	8 2 4	2 5 4	7 1 2	6 7 4	3 5 5	3 5 2
5 4 2	3 5 6	6 3 3	3 0 6	7 3 5	0 9 2	1 2 0	6 5 4
7 8 6	5 8 3	3 7 6	5 2 7	2 5 7	0 4 0	5 2 3	2 2 4
8 8 3	4 4 8	1 1 5	0 6 0	2 2 1	5 6 3	3 3 4	6 8 3
4 8 2	7 5 2	9 3 9	5 9 3	1 7 2	0 7 4	7 3 5	8 8 8
3 0 2	5 8 1	4 7 4	9 5 1	3 6 1	7 5 2	9 6 1	7 4 8
8 7 1	1 8 9	1 9 9	3 5 2	1 3 3	8 2 4	9 1 3	5 3 5
7 7 6	6 1 7	5 8 1	1 3 1	0 8 6	4 8 6	4 0 6	6 2 2
2 6 7	4 6 9	1 6 9	2 3 9	9 0 9	5 3 7	1 7 2	0 8 7
	7 5 3	8 3 3	2 3 4	7 5 5	9 1 4	5 0 9	8 2 5
	5 7 2	6 5 9		4 1 2	6 0 4	0 8 7	4 5 9
	6 9 1			4 1 0		8 3 3	9 8 4
	0 8 8			3 3 1		3 8 5	0 8 9
	8 2 3					1 0 4	3 2 5
	8 2 2					5 6 0	

My observations of the lists of August 18 and June 06 draws led me to my *Category 5* win on June 11. I just thought at betting then, "Why don't <u>all the three of **352**</u> arise after 0 **8 9**?" And they did! But I got half of 5000rur prize because, by a weekly discount, a bet set cost 30 rur.

The small story of the next two June 17 *Category 3*+ *Category 2* exibits is highly informative, too.

LT	WNs	0	1	2	3	4
00:40	6 6 2			•		
00:55	6 5 8					
01:10am	0 1 3	•	•		•	
01:25am	3 6 2			•	•	
01:40am	3 3 1		•		%	

As you can see from the marked draws and the map, according to MOG I expected **3>2>1** in the 3ʳᵈ position of "01:40am" Draw and number **3** in the 1ˢᵗ rather than in the 2ⁿᵈ position. But knowing that "3 - 1" would bring me 1500rur and "-31" 3000rur, I made my choice with the 2ⁿᵈ position. But, being afraid that CHANCE the GIANT would play his innocent joke on me, I filled out a *Category 2* (- 3 1/-1 3) bet set. And He awarded me with the both!

But could I hit "3 3 1" exactly? Yes, look. And you'll see how to hook 2 fish with one hook.

AWESOME!

If, according to MOG, a key-number goes twice in one of the three positions of your expected three WNs, try it and you might

LT	WNs	0	1	2	3	4
00:40	6 6 2			•		
00:55	6 5 8					
01:10am	0 1 3	•	•		•	
01:25am	3 6 2			•	•	
01:40am	3 3 1		•		• •	

get your *Category 6* or even *Category 9* prize if you know the exact position of one of the three WNs.

So, I was impressed to tears by the Beauty of the Outcome.

And even more, this is a remarkable method of hitting TWINNING WNs.

Furthermore, the SM and MOG can help you to hit TOP-3 TRIPLETS like in the last draw below that occurred on June 17, 2019, in the late afternoon.

LT	MNs	0	1	2	3	4	5	6	7	8	9
15:40	2 5 9			●			●				●
15:55	5 3 9				●		●				●
16:10	6 3 2			●	●			●			
16:25	4 3 2			●	●	●					
16:40	2 0 3	●		●	●						
16:55	6 1 0	●	●					●			
17:10	0 0 0	● ● ●									

The crucial idea of this Diamond of CHANCE the GIANT's Collection was the 3rd position where number **0** was expected to appear as a result of right stepped "-1" 2>1>0 diagonal descending.

Then another **0** with its GOLDEN XXX pattern, either in the 1st or 2nd position.

And another **0** as the end of 3>2>1>0 four stepped left descending on the SM.

And where was I at that historic lotto moment? Near the fountain at our local festive square with my second grandkid Daniel.

Imagine how I disappointed CHANCE the GIANT ten days earlier when I didn't hit

888 TRIPLET at 1:55 am on June 08. (It was still June 07 at Moscow Time)

LT	WNs	0	1	2	3	4	5	6	7	8	9
00:55am	**8 8** 9									%	●
01:10am	4 2 5			●		●	●				
01:25am	**8 8** 1		●							%	
01:40am	0 6 0	%					●				
01:55am	**8 8** 8		●		●					% ●	

As you can see, this time you can't conclude from the SM that you must try number **8** in the 3rd position

And I can't understand now why I was so careless and inaccurate and did't support my "88-" bet three times when my notes shows that I paid four 30rur discount bets in the draw, while to get a *Category 9* prize it was enough to spend 300rur on 880, 881,882..88**8**, 889 bet sets.

I suppose it's because it was two hours later after the midnight and sleep was fogging my mind.

The statistics of that draw on the site showed that out of the total 1147 bets there were 89 bets with "888" WNs, 2 bets with "88-" WNs (someone else believed in the twin just once, too) and only two *Category 1* bets, which meant that most of the players wanted more than one or two WNs and became the losers in the end, excepting 89 heroes, me and the one who made a "88-" bet like me.

SM is a good working horse of gaining and collecting *Category 2* prizes when, revealing MOG rules, the map provides you with any 2 WNs and you spend only 3 bet sets on them, grouping them like these:wn1,wn2,– / –,wn1,wn2 / wn1,–,wn2. They are very simple, economical and frequent combinatory wins and, in fact, a stable basement of a player's daily, weekly and monthly wages.

LT	WNs
08:25	7 6 2
08:40	8 6 0
08:55	9 7 9
09:10	3 8 6

Though in this last draw on July 17, 2019 at 09:10 LT you could have *Category 4* prize without SM.

▶ Carefully observing everyday TOP-3 results of draws I have also discovered the whole <u>arithmetic class of simple *Category 2, 3, 4* wins</u> when you get some new WNs by adding +1 or -1 to the WNs in the previous draw like in this 06:10 July 19, 2019 draw.

LT	WNS		
09:55	5	1	2
10:10	**6**	**2**	0
	6(5+1)	**2**(1+1) -	

You just know that it may happen due to correlation between two draws and it does happen sometimes, though it is just an additional means of picking candidates for a new draw when you don't have to save money.

And now I know how to derive a regular benefit from our TOP-3 lottery while it still has such a list of Categories of Prizes.

And I am going to continue my winning path right tomorrow, on August 12, 2019 after sending this manuscript to my Check in iUniverse Coordinator because on our lotto site they offered us a 50% discount on a TOP-3 bet set again. Like a stopped bullet, I had to interrupt my lotto practice for a month to finish the manuscript and I am looking forward to crossing swords with HIS MAJESTY the CHANCE a.s.a.p.

If your TOP-3 lottery has the same or similar categories of prizes and you are in difficulty of guessing how I am going to do it after all my illustrations above and knowing how to use the **C** m/n **formula** for lottery combinations, write to me on ggthefd@gmail.com and I'll be there, for, as usual, I am the first who has to check this elementary combinatory (and more expensive) math technology by myself before offering it to anyone.

Unlike the little builder of the Coral Castle in Florida who for decades erected it secretly, I, fallen in love with and inspired by beautiful Fortuna, CHANCE the GIANT's daughter; I have always built up my Lottery Castle openly, inviting my best friends to look over the enclosure.

PSYCHOLOGICAL ASPECT
OF BIG WINS

I sent my manuscript of the book to my Check in iUniverse Coordinator on August 12, 2019 and, as I told in the previous chapter, I came back to my TOP-3 lotto practice immediately after that.

By 19:25 on August 13 I had logged into my cabinet on our lottery site and written down the results of the last 15 draws on a new page of my grandson's small notepad that was under the PC screen. It has bigger square cells than my old, nearly filled, 2018-19 exercise book.

The WNs of the last three draws were 799, 165 and 551.

LT	WNs		0	1	2	3	4	5	6	7	8	9
19:10	7 9 9									●		%
19:25	1 6 5			●				●	●			
19:40	5 5 1			●				%				

It was clearly seen even without the SM (Spreading Map) that our first two candidates were:

5, as three stepped left triplet;

<u>4</u>, as 6>5>4 vertical correlative descending and 1, as XXX Golden MOG number.

First, I concentrated on 5 and 4 and checked them together like "exactly 54-"(1500RR) in one bet set and— in case they change their positions—"any 54-"(750RR), as you can judge by the wins in the screen of my bets.

And, LOL, I easily hit them spending only 30+30=60RR, while all the three WNs were **5 4 5**.

A	A	A	A	A	A	A	A
2	2	1	2	2	1	2	1
×3	×3	×3	×3	×3	×3	×3	×3
2	2	3	3	3	3	3	3
№ 513	№ 517	№ 514	№ 516	№ 518	№ 598	№ 600	№ 599
1500 P	750 P						

Then, however, there followed my first and second mistakes with them:

1. ***Instead of circling around*** "541" I should have tried "exactly 54-" in, at least, another two twin bet sets because "any 54-" would have guaranteed me 750RR win if they had hit in "45-" position.

2. Assuming, not hesitating and keeping in mind that the Beauty of the Chance could have taken place and exactly "**5 4 –**" would have become WNs, I should have added 0...9 one by one to them, as I had enough money to make a lot of bets. But, under the press of time, my logic of the right betting must have been smashed.

The bitter consolation was in the statistics of the draw results. Out of 1564 bet sets there was just one "not exactly 545" win, mine and someone else's "exactly 54-" wins, mine and someone else's "any 54-" wins.

Точно 3 + Любой 3 (Л3) (2 одинаковых числа)	1	2500	2500
Первые 2 числа	2	1500	3000
Последние 2 числа	0	0	0
Точно 3 + Любой 3 (Л3) (3 разных числа)	0	0	0
Любой порядок 2	2	750	1500

So, in this extremely predictable draw practically only four players (including me) could rely on **5** and **4 WNs** but couldn't make multifold bets on them due to their inner psychological barriers.

«Прости, ОТЕЦ, но что-то я тебя не узнаю...»	"But sorry, FATHER, who are you? I cannot recognize."
«ОДНАКО ЖЕ, КАКОЙ ШЕЛЬМЕЦ, КАКОВ ПРОХВОСТ, НАХАЛ. ТАМ СЛУЧАЙ СНИЗОЙДЁТ К ТЕБЕ ТЫ ОБО МНЕ ПИСАЛ»	WHA-A-AT? YOU FORGO-O-OT? A LIE, PRETENCE! HOW CAN IT EVER BE? *The CHANCE will condescend to you,* YOU WROTE ABOUT ME.
«Когда писал, кому писал?» «НЕ ПОМНИШЬ?» «Краток миг...» «ДА-А, ВЕРНО, ХОТЬ И ПРИВЫКАЛ, ТЫ ТАК И НЕ ПРИВЫК СРЕДИ ЗЕМНОГО РАЗЛИЧАТЬ НЕБЕСНЫЙ ТОНКИЙ ЗНАК, ВПЛОТНУЮ С НИМ ПОДЧАС СТОЯТЬ, В РУКАХ ЕГО ПОЧТИ ДЕРЖАТЬ И БЫТЬ СЛЕПЫМ, ЧУДАК! Я ТОТ, КТО БЫЛ ВСЕГДА С ТОБОЙ, Я СОЛЬ ТВОЕЙ ЛЮБВИ. Я СЛУЧАЙ ТВОЙ, Я ПРИЗРАК ТВОЙ, КАК ХОЧЕШЬ, НАЗОВИ. Я ТОТ, КОМУ ТВОЙ СВЕТ СВЕТИЛ, ТВОЙ ТЕЛЕСКОП ИСКАЛ, КОГДА-ТО НОЧЬЮ СРЕДЬ СВЕТИЛ, В ИЗЛОМАХ КРАСНЫХ СКАЛ...»	"When did I write? To whom I did...? DON'T YOU REMEMBER? "No..." "ATTEMPTING TO BE USED TO IT YOU DIDN'T GET USED, THOUGH, TO MAKING OUT AT A BEND MY HEAVENLY THIN SIGN. AND NEXT TO IT ALMOST TO STAND AND HOLDING TIGHTLY IN YOUR HANDS, YET, BEING BLIND, MY SON. I...I'VE ALWAYS BEEN WITH YOU, IN TRIUMTH ON YOUR FACE. I'M CHANCE OF YOURS. I'M SOUL OF YOURS I'M THOUSANDS OF NAMES. I'M YOUR LAMP, YOUR FIREFLY, LUMINOUS IN THE DARK, YOUR TELESCOPE IN THE NIGHTS, YOUR MAGNIFIER, YOUR BARK..."

Half an hour later my grandson Daniel appeared in the living room and it was impossible to focus on the games already. But I was able to put down 10 more results of the next draws and look at that! *I added one more RULE to MOG, namely, the* *following:*IF A TOP-3 NUMBER DOESN'T HIT FOR A LONG TIME, IT ACCUMULATES ITS HITTING POTENTIAL AND MIGHT HIT, REDUPLICATING OR EVEN TRIPLICATING ITSELF!

LT	WNs	0	1	2	3	4	5	6
	7 9 9	m			m			
	1 6 5	m	●		m		●	●
	5 5 1	m	●		m			
19:55	5 4 5	m			m	●		
	4 7 5	m			m	●		
	6 1 5	m	●		m		●	●
	8 2 1	m	●	●	m			
	4 6 2	m		●	m	●		●
	2 7 4	m		●	m	●		
	7 9 7	m			m			
	9 6 0	●			m			
	8 5 8				m		●	
22:10	9 1 7		●		m			
22:25	3 3 3				●●●			

The statistics of the winning bets in "22:25" Draw showed that there were **21 "exactly three" bets** and only **4 "exactly one" bets**. By correlation, numbers 333 were far from the numbers of the previous "22:10" Draw:917.

To sum up, it meant that there was/were professional player/players who was/were hunting such a UNIQUE OUTCOME.

I eagerly wanted to know whose was or were those 21 winning triplets. What were those players, or, may be, just one person?

No doubt, unlike me, they had privacy at preparing to the draw and betting.

When will I start making my threefold and multifold bets of the SNs which is highly likely to display the Beauty of Chance? This is the question that is still expecting to be answered during my ongoing TOP-3 expansion, because it is of vital importance and necessity, leading me— such a mature lotto player as I am with CHANCE the GIANT and his daughter Fortuna's favor— to my prosperous future.

THE BEAUTY OF THE CHANCE

Having sent my manuscript to iUniverse with my last chapter about psychological problems of big wins I thought that my part of the work had been completed, but on August 17, 2019 at 15:05 LT I received such an amazing evidence of my method of selecting WNs and processing them with my AWMs that I can't help adding another chapter—this one—about the Beauty of the Chance that is suddenly given to you and you must do your best, perhaps, limited by the time again and under any circumstances.

Just before that changing your mind event I sent Derek this email about my two motives of writing the book:

"Such a book is not only my humble contribution to the theory and practice of lottery games but also my gratitude to the English language. In both the aspects it was a challenge and overcoming."

And this is what Derek wrote to me after a while:

"I think you have the 3rd motive Yury>>>and that is to WIN MONEY>>>>it's not enough to analysis and rationalize [and it ain't for fun and a waist of time-but for profit] but the true outcome of ALL this analysis is to win money on a regular basis.

Can you not include the real motive in your story telling?

The rest is an idealist mask. You have to add the money aspect of the WIN...that is the initial offering of your full dedicated analysis work here in your book. That wall is CRACKED and crumbling...remember?"

Yes, it's true.

We had always seen that lotto activity of us a bit differently. I, with CHANCE the GIANT behind me, I saw it more idealistically. But without it I would have lost my ability of surprising at HIS wonderful outcomes and my desire of trying to realize myself fully in the lotto activity long ago. Supergathering of WNs is one of the Highest Miracle of the Lottery World (and not the one that happens only once during your life) and I go through the deepest satisfaction at the time when I am able to make use of it. So, look what happened on that day.

At about 2pm on Sunday, as it was right it, I was sitting in the living room and watching my favorite documentaries on Channel H2 about ancient civilizations when I remembered that I was going to participate in 15:05 Joker game. The wish shaped and rose somewhere from the depth of my consciousness, as it is nearly always with me at the times when something makes me not to skip a draw.

And after 5 minutes—clicking on 24958 and 24959/24958 and 24956/24957 and 24954/24956 and 24952—I was looking at this distribution of these P0, P1, P2 and P3 periodicals:

Almost at once I thought that I would not bet on 46, 47, 48 numbers because they had uniquely played higher in draws 24954 -24957.

I didn't have to click on **F +/- 1** and **F +/- 10** to see that 07, **12, 16, 22 should be under the special control, being left-right stepped slopes** and **01 as 21>11>01 candidate.**

I also decided to include the couple **04-05 because they were a non-periodic couple and, besides, they were "what-after-what" correlating numbers having a double weight both.**

▶ My first row of 13 SNs, wheeled by my Joker AWM for 13, was that: 01-07-12-16-09-35-19-20-40-21-22-24-29

In it I decided to check 19 as the last member of 11-13-15-17 in draw 24959 and 35-40 as Broken Periodicals.

▶ My second row of 17 SNs, wheeled by Joker AWM for 17, was that:01-04-05-07-09-10-12-16-19-20-21-22-24-29-42-43-41 (I didn't place 32 instead of 41,☹)

At about 2:40pm I filled out the bets on the site and went for a walk with my grandson Daniel. We had planned it before and I was in a hurry to leave the stuffy summer flat.

In the evening I saw the result of the draw and was stunned!

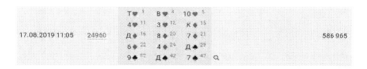

As you can see, by the way, the accumulated Jack Pot was 586 965 rur.

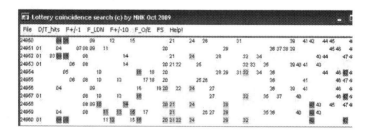

I had a lot of WNs in my two rows among my SNs:

01-07-**12**-**16**-09-35-19-**20**-40-**21**-**22**-**24**-**29**	**8 WNs** in 13 SNs
01-**04**-**05**-07-09-10-**12**-**16**-19-**20**-**21**-**22**-**24**-**29**-**42**-43-41	**11 WNs** in 17 SNs

And my AWMs brought me the 9 wins in every line with the total 1740rur win.

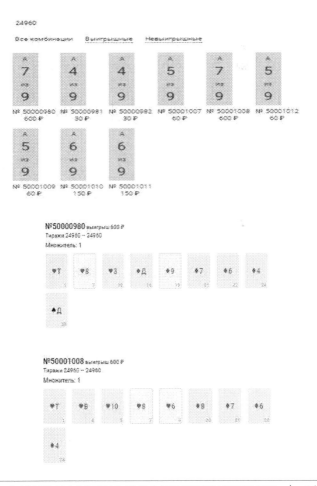

The statistics of the draw on the site showed that out of 1252 bets, beside two mine, there was another 7 in9 win. And that was all, no higher wins than 7 in 9 in that superdraw.

Угаданных чисел	Кол-во победителей	Выигрыш победителя, руб	Общий
9	0	0	0
8	0	0	0
7	3	600	1800
6	16	150	2400
5	71	60	4260
4	235	30	7050

Summing up, for wheeling in my AWMs I selected all the numbers almost perfectly.

But walking with my grandson and kept on thinking at my bets I had an uneasy feeling that I had underdid something.

My two SNs rows show that I was sure in **20-21-22-24-29** rare hitting. I have quite enough similar one-group hittings in my Keno and Joker collection. I was also sure in **12-16.** The similar patterns are scattered in my collection, too. **So, I had 7 WNs in which I was sure!** The problem was with my SNs from the first subdivision:01/04/05/07/09. They had equal chances of hitting.

BUT UNDER THE CIRCUMSTANCES, inner (I could have started analyzing them earlier) and outer (the necessity to go out with my grandson), the idea of checking them in pairs 01-04/04-05/05-07/07-09 didn't come to me, or even trying them preferably with the **04-05** non-periodicals**!**

I stopped thinking about the draw 20 minutes before its 15:05 drawing and the Beauty of the Chance occurred!

Of course, partly glad partly sad, I sent Derek the report and this is what he answered, "*YES great shot Yury>>>very subdued for the Lottery.*"

CONCLUSION

Dear Reader,

The aim of this book is to teach you to be extremely lotto watchful, much luckier in the world of your national lotteries and share your lotto joy with me mentally, or in your email to me or even invite me to your home to celebrate your biggest lottery success.

And when we are luckier, we are happier. And when we are happier we are less aggressive. And when we are less aggressive, the world of the people is a better place to live and to solve collectively our complex ecological, political, religious and overpopulated problems.

From lots of draws of various RF lotteries where personally I didn't participate, in spite of the improbable gathering of WNs, there comes only one MOG+PROG disadvantage.

You have to chase your lottery prey to the very end without a break. When you cannot do that, you should have an assistant, a member of your team, who can double

you just in time when you are very busy, very tired or sick, or on holiday, not to halt the process. I rarely met one, equal to me. And my unhealed wound is that my lotto legacy hasn't become my family business yet.

The grandpa of Starkid, my literary hero in my innovative narrative poem THE BALLAD of STARKID'S CHILDHOOD, SPICED WITH IRREGULAR VERBS written for ESL students of all ages at the end of the last century, an alien from outer space, when parting with his grandson says,

> *"The evolution of mankind*
> *Shows how they fight and fight and fight*
> *Males against males, and kill each other.*
> *Don't ask me why. I'm your grandfather.*
> *I woke you up to say Good-bye.*
> *You've got your spaceship. You can fly.*
> *There, on the Earth, is the reply.*
> *Seeing's believing. Leave and see.*
> *Good luck and…and remember me!"*

And bid him his last farewell.
Kid flung himself round his neck.
His Grandpa tapped him on the back
And wished him,
> *"May the Spacewind swell*
> *Your Starsails! May Cognition Bell*
> *Tolls for you at all your times*
> *Like their Big Ben, or Kremlin Chimes!"*

THE PASS TO MARS AS A GIFT TO MY READERS

And can you guess who its first reader was? Derek, of course. And who were the second ones? His family members and my students in Russia. And the third ones? Definitely, all the iUniverse team who has prepared this book for its publication and who, reminding me of that kindly, since 2013, for nearly 7 years, had patiently been pushing me to my final decision to generalize my lotto achievements and to dare to present them to all the lotto public in English speaking countries.

You see, Mars has also been in me since my high school years when with a school telescope, given me on trust by our Physics teacher Albina Mercurievna, I explored the night sky, the Moon and the planets. I am even closer to it now, as my niece, her husband and their elder son have been working for the Gagarin's Cosmonauts Training Center under Moscow.

"21.12.2018

Hi, dear Derek and all your nearest and dearest! Merry Christmas and to the occasion this is my new Christmas creation as a romantic application and a treat to your Special Relativity Theory Certificate.

It has become my tradition to carefully pick out something from our Russian Top Pop Songs Collection and translate a piece of lyric into English. Each time it's a challange to me. And again I hope I've coped with it and my another tiny masterpiece is here to entertain you.

THIS SONG is one of our cosmonauts' favourite. Appearing in the early 1960s, it has been always popular with them. I like the clarity and the lightness of the performer's voice.

In Russian it is called AND ON MARS APPLE TREES WILL BE IN BLOSSOM

Жить и верить - это замечательно. Перед нами небывалые пути. Утверждают космонавты и мечтатели, Что на Марсе будут яблони цвести.	To live and to believe, this is wonderful. Before us there are fabulous paths. Cosmonauts and Dreamers state That apple trees will bloom on Mars.
Хорошо, когда с тобой товарищи. Всю Вселенную объехать и пройти. Звёзды встретятся с Землёю расцветающей И на Марсе будут яблони цвести.	It's good when friends are there, Travelling and hiking across the Universe. Stars will see the florishing Earth, And apple trees will bloom on Mars.
Я со звёздами сдружился дальними. Не волнуйся обо мне и не грусти. Покидая нашу Землю, обещали мы. Что на Марсе будут яблони цвести.	I've made friends with distant stars. Don't worry about me and don't be sad. Leaving our Earth, we were promising That apple trees would bloom on Mars.

In English I made it much more universal, breathing a new life into this historic song.

Living and believing what's more wonderful?
We are moving to another cosmic boom.
Categoric, space explorers and all astronauts
That on Mars, its own apple trees will bloom.
Categoric, space biologists and cosmonauts

That on Mars, its Martian apple trees will bloom.

Sounds great when there are friends around you,
With the close Universe like 'n opened tomb.
Just a superhuman effort in next breaking through,
And on Mars our earthly apple trees will bloom.
Just a Herculean effort in the next breakthrough,
And on Mars our apple trees will shortly bloom.

I'm appealed by distant suns from far away.
Don't worry; never plunge your hearts in gloom.
Leaving our Solar System we were promising
That new planets would be dressed in apple bloom.
Leaving every Solar System we are promising
That new planets will be dressed in apple bloom.

Having Faith and Being what's more marvellous?
We are streaming to the greatest AI boom.
Optimistic, Earth's florists and all pharmacists:
Apple blossoms Martian air will perfume.
Optimistic, Earth's dreamers and astronomers
Apple blossoms Martian air will resume.

ENJOY my OWN singing as an attempt of its first presentation in English. HAVE a NICE TIME singing it together with your grandkids."

And Derek was quick in reply.

"Hello Yury>>>that was a nice pleasant surprise to hear your singing and the great Russian voice of that baritone. I like it very much. And glad you translated...I needed it! LOLOL.

You should sing your poetry!!! You have a great sullen deep voice for the mellow dramatics.

We will be in Montreal for several days...trust the weather holds.

Merry Christmas to you too and all your family and friends."

This is the link to the song with the baritone Derek mentions:https://yandex.ru/search/?text=в.трошин.%20и%20на%20марсе%20будут%20яблони%20цвести&clid=2055854&win=227&lr=237#/videowiz?filmId=17294484530224856166

Or this trio of younger performers:
https://www.youtube.com/watch?v=zbTIymCKCW4
https://youtu.be/zbTIymCKCW4

Printed in the United States
By Bookmasters